THE WRITER'S COMPASS

50 Tips to Help Navigate Your Storytelling Journey

Michael Mammarella

ABOUT THE AUTHOR

MICHAEL MAMMARELLA

Michael Mammarella is a writer, screenwriter, and storyteller with a passion for crafting compelling narratives and immersive worlds. A graduate of the Queensland College of Art, he has explored a range of storytelling mediums and experienced both the triumphs and challenges of the creative process. Drawing from his experiences, he is dedicated to helping fellow writers overcome challenges, while also unlocking their full creative potential.

Copyright © 2025 Michael Mammarella

All rights reserved.

ISBN: 978-1-7640198-3-5

DEDICATION

This book is for the storytellers. It's for the dreamers who turn fleeting ideas into worlds, who chase inspiration even when it feels out of reach, and who understand that every story — no matter how messy — deserves to be told.

It's for the writers staring at a blank page, feeling stuck, but knowing deep down that their story is worth telling.

Consider this your guide, your pep talk, and your reminder that every great story starts with a writer who refuses to quit.

Now, let's get writing.

CONTENTS

INTRODUCTION. / **PAGE 1**

PART 1: THE WRITER'S MINDSET.

TIP 1 : *The 3 P's of Writing Success – Persistence, Patience, and Perfection.* / ***PAGE 4***

TIP 2 : *How to Beat Writer's Block (Without Throwing Your Laptop Out the Window).* / ***PAGE 5***

TIP 3 : *4 Ways to Avoid Overwriting: Keep Your Reader's Attention.* / ***PAGE 8***

TIP 4 : *The Secret Method to Writing Fast and Maximizing Productivity.* / ***PAGE 12***

TIP 5 : *How to Create a Killer First Line.* / ***PAGE 13***

PART 2: THE WRITING PROCESS.

TIP 6 : *Stop Overthinking! The Power of 'Just Write'.* / ***PAGE 19***

TIP 7 : *Editing vs. Writing: When to Switch Gears.* / ***PAGE 21***

TIP 8 : *5 Editing Mistakes Every Writer Makes (And How to Fix Them).* / ***PAGE 23***

TIP 9 : *Why You Shouldn't Be Afraid to Kill Your Darlings.* / ***PAGE 27***

TIP 10 : *The Best Writing Apps You Didn't Know You Needed.* / ***PAGE 29***

PART 3: STAYING MOTIVATED AND INSPIRED.

TIP 11 : *How to Stay Motivated When You Don't Feel Like Writing.* **/ PAGE 34**

TIP 12 : *How to Avoid Clichés in Your Writing.* **/ PAGE 35**

TIP 13: *The Power of Writing Prompts.* **/ PAGE 41**

TIP 14 : *How to Use Feedback to Improve Your Writing.* **/ PAGE 45**

TIP 15 : *How to Develop Strong Characters That Readers Will Love.* **/ PAGE 50**

PART 4: MASTERING STORYTELLING TECHNIQUES.

TIP 16 : *The Importance of Dialogue in Storytelling.* **/ PAGE 57**

TIP 17 : *How to Write a Scene That Keeps Your Readers Hooked.* **/ PAGE 62**

TIP 18 : *How to Create Tension in Your Writing.* **/ PAGE 67**

TIP 19 : *The Benefits of Writing Every Day (Even Just for 10 Minutes).* **/ PAGE 71**

TIP 20 : *The Best Time to Write: Morning, Noon, or Night?* **/ PAGE 73**

PART 5: FINDING BALANCE AS A WRITER.

TIP 21 : *How to Balance Writing with a Busy Life.* **/ PAGE 76**

TIP 22 : *The Power of a Writing Routine.* **/ PAGE 77**

TIP 23 : *Writing with Emotion: How to Make Your Readers Feel Something.* **/ PAGE 79**

TIP 24 : *Writing from Real Life: How to Turn Your Experiences into Stories.* **/ PAGE 84**

TIP 25 : *How to Craft the Perfect Ending.* **/ PAGE 86**

PART 6: ADVANCED WRITING SKILLS.

TIP 26 : *How to Write Conflict That Moves the Plot Forward.* **/ PAGE 92**

TIP 27 : *The Art of Subtext in Writing: What's Left Unsaid.* **/ PAGE 97**

TIP 28 : *How to Write a Compelling Villain.* **/ PAGE 101**

TIP 29 : *Why Writers Need to Read (And What to Read).* **/ PAGE 107**

TIP 30 : *How to Write a Strong Opening Scene.* **/ PAGE 108**

PART 7: STRUCTURE AND STYLE.

TIP 31 : *How to Use Flashbacks Without Confusing Your Reader.* **/ PAGE 115**

TIP 32 : *How to Write Realistic Dialogue.* **/ PAGE 120**

TIP 33 : *How to Overcome Writer's Block.* **/ PAGE 125**

TIP 34 : *The Importance of Editing and Revising.* **/ PAGE 127**

TIP 35 : *How to Write a Strong Protagonist.* **/ PAGE 128**

PART 8: KEEPING READERS ENGAGED.

TIP 36 : *How to Write a Plot Twist.* / ***PAGE 135***

TIP 37 : *How to Write Suspense and Keep Readers on the Edge of Their Seat.* / ***PAGE 140***

TIP 38 : *How to Stay Inspired as a Writer.* / ***PAGE 146***

TIP 39 : *How to Write Romantic Relationships in Your Story.* / ***PAGE 151***

TIP 40 : *How to Write an Effective Opening Hook.* / ***PAGE 157***

PART 9: MASTERING THE FINAL ELEMENTS OF YOUR STORY.

TIP 41 : *How to Write a Memorable Villain.* / ***PAGE 165***

TIP 42 : *How to Build World-Building in Fiction.* / ***PAGE 170***

TIP 43 : *The Power of Setting: How to Create Atmosphere in Your Story.* / ***PAGE 176***

TIP 44 : *How to Write a Prologue That Sets the Stage.* / ***PAGE 182***

TIP 45 : *Writing for Different Genres: Tips for Every Type of Writer.* / ***PAGE 188***

PART 10: PERFECTING YOUR CRAFT AND MOVING FORWARD.

TIP 46 : *How to Write an Emotional Story Arc.* / ***PAGE 197***

TIP 47 : *The Art of Foreshadowing: Planting Clues for Your Readers.* / ***PAGE 204***

TIP 48 : *Writing Strong Female Characters: How to Make Them Complex and Real.* **/ PAGE 210**

TIP 49 : *The Importance of Pacing in Your Story.* **/ PAGE 217**

TIP 50 : *How to Write a Story That Resonates with Your Audience.* **/ PAGE 224**

CONCLUSION. **/ PAGE 231**

NOTE FROM THE AUTHOR. **/ PAGE 232**

INTRODUCTION

Welcome to *The Writer's Compass: 50 Tips to Help Navigate Your Creative Journey*. Writing is an adventure filled with inspiration, challenges, and self-discovery. Whether you are just beginning your writing journey or are an experienced storyteller seeking fresh insights, this book is designed to serve as your guide, offering practical advice, motivation, and strategies to keep you moving forward.

In the pages ahead, you will find 50 carefully crafted tips that address common struggles writers face, from overcoming writer's block and refining storytelling techniques to developing strong characters and mastering the art of editing. These insights aim to help you build confidence, improve your craft, and establish a writing routine that works for you.

SOME KEY AREAS COVERED INCLUDE:

MINDSET AND MOTIVATION: Discover how persistence, patience, and a willingness to embrace imperfection can lead to writing success.

PRODUCTIVITY HACKS: Learn methods like the Pomodoro Technique to help maximize efficiency and stay consistent in your writing practice.

STORYTELLING ESSENTIALS: Find out how to craft compelling first lines, create memorable characters, and write gripping plot twists that keep readers engaged.

OVERCOMING COMMON PITFALLS: Avoid common mistakes like overwriting, weak dialogue, and clichés that can weaken your storytelling.

THE POWER OF EDITING: Understand when to switch from writing to editing and how to refine your work for clarity, impact, and emotional resonance.

Each tip is presented in a concise and accessible format, allowing you to apply the advice immediately. Whether you need a quick burst of inspiration or a structured approach to refining your craft, this book provides actionable guidance tailored to all stages of the writing process.

Writing is a journey, not a destination, and every word you put on the page brings you closer to your goals. With *The Writer's Compass* as your guide, you will have the tools and encouragement needed to navigate the creative process with confidence and clarity.

Now, let's embark on this journey together, one word at a time.

PART 1: THE WRITER'S MINDSET

This section lays the foundation for success by focusing on the mental resilience needed to thrive as a writer. It covers the importance of "The 3 P's of Writing Success" and provides strategies to overcome self-doubt, perfectionism, and fear of failure. Writers will also learn how to embrace imperfection, develop discipline, and stay committed to their creative journey, regardless of setbacks.

TIP 1. THE 3 P'S OF WRITING SUCCESS

Writing isn't just about talent, it's about commitment. No great novel, screenplay, or short story is written in a single inspired burst. Every writer faces challenges, rejections, creative slumps, and self-doubt. But those who push through, who keep writing even when it feels impossible, are the ones who grow. Persistence keeps you going despite obstacles, patience reminds you that good writing takes time, and progress ensures that every word, every draft, and every struggle moves you closer to mastery. Here's how the 3 P's can help you succeed:

1. Persistence.

Writing isn't always easy, and some days the words just don't come. But persistence is key! Keep writing, even when it feels tough, even when you feel stuck. The more you write, the more you'll improve. Every word you write brings you one step closer to your goal. Whether it's 10 minutes or 10 hours, writing consistently is what builds a successful writing practice. Remember, the best writers don't quit when it gets hard, they keep going.

2. Patience.

Great writing takes time. You won't perfect your craft overnight, and that's okay! Be patient with yourself. Sometimes your ideas will need to marinate, your first draft will need revising, and your voice will evolve. Instead of rushing through, trust that every step of the process contributes to your growth. Writing is a marathon, not a sprint. So, embrace the journey and give yourself the time you need to refine your work.

3. Perfection.

Writing isn't about perfection on the first try, it's about progress. Editing and improving your work often takes multiple drafts. The first draft doesn't have to be flawless, and sometimes you won't know what works until you've written it out and gone back to revise. Embrace the process of refining, tweaking, and perfecting. Remember: Perfection is achieved through consistent effort and continuous improvement.

Every step you take, no matter how small, is progress on your writing journey. Whether you're facing doubts or pushing through writer's block, keep going. It's all part of the process!

TIP 2. HOW TO BEAT WRITER'S BLOCK (WITHOUT THROWING YOUR LAPTOP OUT THE WINDOW)

Writer's block is the worst, but don't stress, you're not alone! We've all been there. Here's how to break through it to get your creativity flowing again:

1. Take a 10-Minute Break.

When you're staring at a blank page with no words coming, sometimes the best thing you can do is step away. Our brains aren't meant to be in constant problem-solving mode, and when we push too hard, we can actually block creative ideas from forming.

Taking a 10-minute break resets your mental state and allows your subconscious to work through the problem in the background. During this time, try:

- **Stretching** to release tension in your body (which can also release mental tension).

- **Take a walk** to get fresh air and change your surroundings.

- **Listening to music** to shift your mood and engage a different part of your brain.

- **Practicing deep breathing** to calm frustration and reset your focus.

The key is to detach from the writing process briefly so that when you return, you're approaching it with fresh energy and a clear mind. Often, the solution to writer's block isn't forcing words onto the page. It's giving your brain the chance to find them on its own.

2. Change Your Writing Space.

Your environment can have a huge impact on your creativity. If you always write in the same place and feel stuck, a simple shift in location can reignite inspiration.

Try moving to:

- **A coffee shop** where the hum of people can provide background energy.

- **A park or outdoor space** to let nature refresh your perspective.

- **A different room in your house** — even sitting on the floor instead of a desk can shift your mindset.

- **A library or co-working space** for a fresh but focused atmosphere.

Our brains associate spaces with specific activities. If you always write at your desk where you also check emails or do work, your brain might struggle to switch into a creative mode. Changing locations signals a mental reset and can help you view your writing from a fresh angle.

3. Write Anything, Even Nonsense!

One of the biggest causes of writer's block is the pressure to be perfect. Instead of waiting for the "right" words, let yourself write anything — even if it's complete nonsense.

Some techniques to loosen up your writing:

- **Freewriting:** Set a timer for five or ten minutes and write nonstop, no matter what. Even if you're just typing "I don't know what to write" over and over, you're breaking the cycle of being stuck.

- **Writing prompts:** Use a random prompt to start a new paragraph or scene — sometimes shifting focus can reignite inspiration for your main project.

- **Describe something ordinary:** Write about the cup on your desk, the sound outside your window, or what you had for breakfast. The act of writing *anything* gets your mind warmed up.

- **Write bad on purpose:** Challenge yourself to write the worst, most ridiculous version of your scene. You'll likely find it frees up creativity and gives you something real to work with.

The goal isn't to create a masterpiece — it's to break through resistance. Once you get words flowing, your brain will naturally start shaping them into something more structured and meaningful.

TIP 3. 4 WAYS TO AVOID OVERWRITING: KEEP YOUR READER'S ATTENTION

Overwriting is one of the quickest ways to lose a reader's interest. Bloated sentences, excessive description, and redundant phrasing can slow down the pacing and make a story feel clunky or unfocused. Good writing isn't about using the most words, it's about using the *right* words.

Try these techniques to streamline your writing, strengthen your storytelling, and maintain momentum in your work:

1. Keep Sentences Concise & Avoid Redundant Descriptions.

Long, winding sentences can confuse or bore your reader, making it difficult to stay engaged. Aim for clarity and brevity by keeping sentences tight and purposeful. Every word should earn its place on the page.

Instead of: *"She walked slowly and cautiously through the dark, eerie hallway, her footsteps barely making a sound as she moved forward."*

Try: *"She crept through the dark hallway, her footsteps silent."*

Instead of: *"He sat down in the chair and rested his hands on the table, looking at her with an intense, serious gaze."*

Try: *"He sat, hands on the table, eyes locked on hers."*

How to fix it:

1. Eliminate filler words (*that, just, really, very, in order to*).
2. Don't restate what's already obvious (*He shrugged his shoulders → He shrugged*).
3. Avoid repeating descriptions—if you've already described a setting or a character, don't rehash it unless it's necessary.

Pro Tip: Every sentence should move the story forward. If it doesn't, it's probably worth cutting.

2. Show, Don't Tell.

Readers want to experience a story, not just be told about it. Instead of stating emotions or actions outright, let readers infer them through context, behavior, and sensory details. Show the actions : like the character biting her nails, tapping her foot, or stuttering. This technique pulls readers in and allows them to experience the story for themselves.

Instead of: *"She was nervous about her big speech."*

Try: *"She tightened her grip on her notes, her foot tapping an uneven rhythm beneath the podium."*

Instead of: *"He was furious."*

Try: *"His fists clenched, his jaw tightened, and his breath came in short bursts."*

How to Fix It:

1. Use body language, tone, and actions to convey emotions.
2. Let dialogue and reactions reveal character dynamics instead of explaining them.
3. Incorporate sensory details (sight, sound, touch, taste, smell) to immerse the reader.

Pro Tip: If you can replace "felt" or "was" with an action or description, you're on the right track!

3. Use Active Voice.

Active voice creates energy, urgency, and clarity, while passive voice often makes writing feel sluggish and distant. It makes the subject the doer of the action, which keeps the writing clear and engaging.

Instead of: *"The book was placed on the shelf by Sarah."*

Try: *"Sarah placed the book on the shelf."*

Instead of: *"A decision was made by the board to delay the project."*

Try: *"The board decided to delay the project."*

How to Fix It:

1. Make the subject of the sentence the one performing the action.
2. Look for passive constructions (*was written, was given, was made*) and rework them when possible.
3. Passive voice has its place, but too much of it can create a detached tone.

Pro Tip: Active voice makes writing sharper and more engaging — use it whenever possible.

4. Cut Unnecessary Adverbs.

Adverbs (*quickly, suddenly, very, really*) can weaken writing when they replace a stronger verb. Instead of propping up weak verbs with adverbs, use precise and vivid language.

Instead of: *"She ran very quickly to the car."*

Try: *"She sprinted to the car."*

Instead of: *"He spoke loudly and angrily."*

Try: *He shouted.*

How to Fix It:

1. Replace adverbs with stronger verbs (*walked slowly → crept, ran quickly → sprinted*).
2. Keep adverbs that change the meaning of a sentence, but cut the ones that add unnecessary fluff.
3. Trust your verbs—they should do the heavy lifting.

Pro Tip: If you remove an adverb and the sentence still conveys the same meaning, you probably don't need it.

TIP 4. THE SECRET METHOD TO WRITING FAST AND MAXIMIZING PRODUCTIVITY

This method, known as the **Pomodoro Technique**, is perfect for anyone who struggles with distractions or writer's block. Here's how it works:

1. Set a Timer For 25 Minutes.

The key is focusing for a set amount of time. 25 minutes might feel short, but it's the perfect duration to get into a flow state. During this time, you eliminate distractions, silence your phone, and commit to writing without checking social media or overthinking. You're essentially setting a "deadline" for your brain to be super focused. This bursts the mental block and makes the task feel more manageable!

2. Write Non-Stop.

This is where the magic happens. Once the timer starts, write as much as you can, and don't worry about spelling, grammar, or perfection. Just get the words flowing. The pressure of time creates a sense of urgency, helping you push through any hesitations. Don't stop until the timer goes off — if you get stuck, just write whatever comes to mind and keep your momentum going. The goal is productivity, not perfection!

3. Take a 5-Minute Break.

After 25 minutes of intense focus, your brain needs a quick reset. Take a 5-minute break to stretch, walk around, grab a drink, or just relax. This small break helps you avoid burnout, recharge, and return to your next writing session with fresh energy. This consistent cycle of work and rest is what keeps you productive without feeling overwhelmed.

Whether you're tackling a short story, an article, or a novel, the Pomodoro Technique is a game changer and makes writing faster and more enjoyable.

TIP 5. HOW TO CREATE A KILLER FIRST LINE

Your first line is your story's handshake, its first impression, and its promise to the reader. It's the moment where someone decides whether they're going to keep turning the page—or set your book down and walk away. A killer first line grabs attention, sparks curiosity, and pulls the reader into your world before they even realize it.

Think about some of the most iconic first lines in literature:

"It was a bright cold day in April, and the clocks were striking thirteen." – *1984* by George Orwell

"Call me Ishmael." – *Moby-Dick* by Herman Melville

"The man in black fled across the desert, and the gunslinger followed." – *The Gunslinger* by Stephen King

These lines ignite intrigue, establish tone, and set up the journey ahead, all within a handful of words. But what makes them so powerful?

Here are three essential techniques to craft a first line that hooks your reader instantly:

1. Keep It Intriguing.

A great first line makes readers ask a question, one that demands an answer. It can be a contradiction, a strange occurrence, a bold statement, or a unique perspective. Whatever it is, it should pull the reader forward and make them wonder, *what happens next?*

Examples of intriguing first lines:

- *"It was the best of times, it was the worst of times..."* – *A Tale of Two Cities* by Charles Dickens
- *"All children, except one, grow up."* – *Peter Pan* by J.M. Barrie
- *"You better not never tell nobody but God."* – *The Color Purple* by Alice Walker

These lines instantly create a sense of mystery, contradiction, or tension, urging the reader to keep going. The goal is to ignite curiosity and leave them wanting more.

How to apply this:

- Start with an unexpected statement that forces readers to question what they just read.

- Introduce a character, situation, or conflict that hints at something bigger.

- Use a contradiction that makes readers think.

2. Make It Emotional.

Readers connect with emotions before they connect with a plot. A first line that immediately tugs at their feelings will grab attention because it feels personal. Whether it's longing, nostalgia, humor, fear, or grief, emotions make a first line powerful and relatable.

Examples of emotional first lines:

- *"In my younger and more vulnerable years, my father gave me some advice that I've been turning over in my mind ever since." – The Great Gatsby* by F. Scott Fitzgerald
- *"I write this sitting in the kitchen sink." – I Capture the Castle* by Dodie Smith
- *"It was a pleasure to burn." – Fahrenheit 451* by Ray Bradbury

Each of these lines immediately immerses you in the character's mindset or emotions. They make you feel nostalgic, uneasy, or even amused, but most importantly, they make you care.

How to apply this:

- Start with an internal reflection or a moment of vulnerability.

- Show a character's mindset before revealing their situation.

- Use sensory details to evoke a specific mood.

3. Set the Tone or Mystery.

Your first line should reflect the mood and style of your story. A thriller might begin with an eerie statement, while a comedy might open with something absurd. Alternatively, mystery hooks the reader by introducing a puzzle or question that needs an answer.

Examples of tone-setting and mysterious first lines:

- *"Mr. and Mrs. Dursley, of number four, Privet Drive, were proud to say that they were perfectly normal, thank you very much."* – Harry Potter and the Sorcerer's Stone by J. K. Rowling (light, whimsical tone)
- *"This is the saddest story I have ever heard."* – The Good Soldier by Ford Madox Ford (melancholic, dramatic tone)
- *"They shoot the white girl first."* – Paradise by Toni Morrison (mysterious, shocking tone)

If your story is suspenseful, tragic, humorous, or eerie, let your first line set that expectation.

How to apply this:

- If your book is dark, make your first line unsettling.
- If your book is humorous, start with a quirky observation or absurdity.
- If your book is mysterious, introduce an unanswered question right away.

A killer first line doesn't have to be complicated, it just needs to be intentional. Whether it intrigues, creates an emotional connection, or sets the tone, it should compel your reader to keep turning pages.

Next time you sit down to write, ask yourself:

- *Does my first line create curiosity?*
- *Does it engage emotion?*
- *Does it establish the tone of my story?*

If the answer is *yes*, then you're on your way to crafting an unforgettable opening.

PART 2: THE WRITING PROCESS

Writing is more than just putting words on a page. It's about developing a system that works for you. This section explores methods to beat writer's block, optimize creativity, and maximize productivity. It also covers drafting strategies, the importance of separating writing from editing, and how to cultivate a consistent writing routine that fosters progress.

TIP 6. STOP OVERTHINKING! THE POWER OF 'JUST WRITE'

Stop overthinking, JUST WRITE!

We've all been there, staring at a blank page or blinking cursor, feeling overwhelmed by the pressure to make every word perfect. But here's the truth: perfection can come later. The most important thing is to get started. So, stop stressing about every little detail and just let your ideas flow.

Here's why you should embrace the 'Just Write' mindset:

1. Perfection Can Come Later.

One of the biggest mistakes writers make is trying to craft a masterpiece on the first attempt. The pressure to write something flawless can stop you from writing *anything* at all.

Think of your first draft as raw material. It doesn't have to be polished, structured, or even make complete sense. The goal is to get your ideas onto the page, so you have something to work with. Many of the greatest writers will tell you: "You can't edit a blank page."

- **Give yourself permission to write badly.** No one is judging your first draft, and you'll refine it later.

- **Write like no one is watching.** The more you detach from the need for perfection, the easier it becomes to let creativity take the lead.

- **Remember: Editing is where the magic happens.** Your focus now is just to *write*.

In the end, the key is to get your thoughts onto the page without the expectation that they'll be perfect from the start. Once the ideas are there, you can go back and shape them into something amazing.

2. Momentum Is Key.

Writing isn't just about skill, it's about momentum. Once you start writing, your brain naturally falls into a rhythm, making it easier to keep going. The hardest part is often just *starting*.

- **Set a timer for 10-15 minutes** and commit to writing non-stop. You might be surprised how quickly the words start flowing.

- **Don't pause to edit.** Every time you stop to tweak a sentence; you interrupt your creative flow. Keep moving forward and refine later.

- **Push past resistance.** The first few sentences may feel stiff, but the more you write, the more natural it becomes.

Momentum is what separates writers who finish their work from those who never get past the first paragraph. Once you get words on the page, the rest will follow.

3. You Can Always Edit, But You Can't Edit a Blank Page!

If you struggle with overthinking, remind yourself of this simple truth: A rough draft can be improved, but a blank page can't.

- **Think of your first draft as a blueprint.** It doesn't have to be pretty — it just needs to exist.

- **Embrace the messy draft.** Many successful authors write entire novels that start as chaotic, unstructured thoughts. The refining happens in later drafts.
- **Trust the process.** Writing is a journey, and every draft brings you one step closer to the story you want to tell.

The goal isn't to write something perfect, it's to write something, period. Once you have words on the page, you have something to shape, refine, and turn into a compelling piece of work.

TIP 7. EDITING VS. WRITING: WHEN TO SWITCH GEARS

As writers, it's easy to get caught in the trap of editing while we write. But here's the thing: writing and editing require different mindsets, and trying to do both at the same time will slow you down.

Let the ideas flow freely without worrying about perfection. Once you've got everything down, then it's time to shift into editing mode. Here's when to switch gears:

1. Write First. Focus on Getting Your Story Out.

When you're in the writing phase, your main objective is to get your story, characters, and ideas onto the page. This is the creative stage, where your focus should be on flow, energy, and storytelling, not perfection.

- **Don't edit as you go.** Stopping to tweak sentences can kill momentum and make writing feel tedious.

- **Let ideas evolve naturally.** Some of your best thoughts will only come once you've written the first draft.

- **Embrace imperfection.** Your first draft is meant to be raw. Clunky sentences, weak descriptions, and awkward dialogue can be fixed later.

Think of writing like sculpting — you need to gather the raw material first before you can chisel it into something refined. If you stop every few words to polish, you risk never finishing the draft at all.

2. Edit Later. Revisions Come After You Have the Full Picture.

Once your draft is complete, it's time to switch from creator to editor. This is where you step back and analyze your work with fresh eyes, looking for ways to improve clarity, structure, and impact.

- **Focus on the big picture first.** Before fixing minor typos, assess whether your plot flows well, your characters are compelling, and your scenes have purpose.

- **Separate writing from editing sessions.** Give yourself time between drafting and editing so you can approach your work objectively.

- **Break edits into stages.** Start with structural changes (plot, pacing, character arcs) before fine-tuning dialogue, grammar, and word choice.

Editing allows you to shape your story into something powerful, but only after you have something solid to work with. Trying to perfect every sentence before the draft is done will slow you down and may even cause you to lose sight of the bigger picture.

3. Why Switching Gears Matters.

When you try to write and edit at the same time, you're constantly interrupting your own creative process. Writing requires fluidity, exploration, and allowing ideas to unfold, while editing demands precision, critique, and refinement. If you mix the two, you may find yourself:

- **Spending hours on a single paragraph** instead of finishing a chapter.

- **Losing your creative spark** because you're too focused on minor errors.

- **Struggling to make progress** because you keep second-guessing every sentence.

By committing to writing first and editing later, you give yourself permission to write freely without fear of "messing up." And when it's time to edit, you can fully focus on improving your work without being distracted by unfinished ideas.

TIP 8. 5 EDITING MISTAKES EVERY WRITER MAKES (AND HOW TO FIX THEM)

Editing mistakes can sneak past even the most seasoned writers! Whether you're revising a blog post, a novel, or just a short story, it's easy to overlook common issues that can make your writing weaker. Here are 5 editing mistakes you want to watch out for:

1. Overusing Adverbs – Cut Them Down!

Adverbs (*quickly, really, very, suddenly*) can be useful, but they often signal weak writing. Instead of propping up weak verbs with adverbs, replace them with stronger, more specific verbs.

Instead of: *She ran very quickly.*
Try: *She sprinted.*

Instead of: *He spoke loudly and angrily.*
Try: *He shouted.*

How to fix it:

1. Do a **search for adverbs** in your manuscript (words ending in "-ly").
2. Ask yourself: *Can I use a more precise verb instead?*
3. If the adverb is truly necessary, keep it, but most of the time, it can be cut without losing meaning.

2. Wordiness – Keep It Concise!

Many writers fall into the trap of using too many words to say something simple. Long-winded sentences can muddy your writing and distract readers from your main point. The best writing is clear, direct, and efficient.

Instead of: *Due to the fact that he was tired, he decided to take a nap.*
Try: *Since he was tired, he took a nap.*

Instead of: *She was the kind of person who always went out of her way to help others in any possible way.*
Try: *She always helped others.*

How to fix it:

1. Read sentences aloud. If they feel clunky or too long, trim them.
2. Look for redundant phrases. (*"absolutely essential," "unexpected surprise," "basic fundamentals"*)
3. Ask: Can I say this in fewer words?

3. Passive Voice – Make It Active!

Passive voice makes sentences less direct and engaging. It often buries the subject and weakens the action. Active voice is clearer, stronger, and more compelling.

Instead of: *The book was read by her.*
Try: *She read the book.*

Instead of: *A decision was made by the committee.*
Try: *The committee made a decision.*

How to fix it:

1. Look for "was" + past participle (*was written, was seen, was done*).
2. Rewrite in active voice when possible—make the subject perform the action.
3. Passive voice isn't always wrong, but overuse can make writing feel weak or distant.

4. Repetitive Words – Mix It Up!

Using the same words or phrases repeatedly can make writing feel monotonous. Readers may lose engagement if they notice patterns in your wording.

Instead of: *She looked at the door. She looked at the clock. She looked down at her hands.*
Try: *She glanced at the door, checked the clock, then dropped her gaze to her hands.*

Instead of: *The dark forest loomed ahead. The dark path wound through the trees. The dark sky stretched above.*
Try: *The shadowy forest loomed ahead, its winding path snaking through dense trees beneath an ink-black sky.*

How to fix it:

1. Use a thesaurus but be careful not to overcomplicate things. Don't fill your stories with words the reader can't pronounce or doesn't understand.
2. Read your work aloud to catch repetition.
3. Vary sentence structure to avoid repeating patterns.

5. Lack Of Structure – Ensure Flow!

Even if your writing is polished, a lack of structure can make it feel disjointed. Every paragraph should logically lead into the next, creating a smooth reading experience.

Instead of: *"The detective found a clue. Earlier, he had spoken to a witness. He was sure the case was closing in."*
Try: *"After speaking to the witness, the detective discovered a crucial clue. Now, he was sure — the case was closing in."*

How to fix it:

1. Make sure your ideas flow logically. One thought should lead to the next.
2. Use transition words (*however, therefore, meanwhile, next*) to connect ideas.
3. Check paragraph structure. Each paragraph should focus on one clear idea.

TIP 9. WHY YOU SHOULDN'T BE AFRAID TO KILL YOUR DARLINGS

One of the hardest things for any writer is cutting a scene, character, or passage that they love. These are the moments we feel most attached to, but if they don't serve the story, they can actually weaken it. Killing your darlings isn't about sacrificing creativity; it's about refining your work into its sharpest, strongest form. Here's why you shouldn't be afraid to let go:

1. It Strengthens Your Story.

Every element in your writing should serve a purpose, whether it moves the plot forward, develops a character, or deepens the theme. If you're attached to something but it doesn't actually move the plot forward, or contribute to character development, it might be time to cut it. Remember, by removing distractions, you give your readers a more focused, compelling narrative.

- Ask yourself: *Does this scene contribute to the overall arc?*
- If you removed this section, *would the story still make sense?*
- Is it slowing the pacing, creating unnecessary distractions, or over-explaining something?

By cutting what isn't needed, you tighten the narrative, making the story more engaging and immersive for readers. A sharper story is a stronger story.

2. Less Is More. Every Word Should Serve the Characters or Plot.

Sometimes, we get attached to clever phrases, beautiful descriptions, or unique ideas, but that doesn't mean they belong in your story. If a "darling" doesn't advance the plot or develop your characters, it's just taking up precious space. Every word in your work should have a purpose.

- A beautifully written paragraph that doesn't add anything meaningful can slow the reader down.
- A scene that's emotionally rich but doesn't develop the character's journey might be better as backstory, not main text.
- A line of dialogue that's clever but doesn't advance the plot, is just cleverness for the sake of cleverness.

By removing excess, you streamline the story, allowing what truly matters to shine through.

3. Letting Go Leads to Better Work.

Writing is about evolution. The first draft is where you let everything out, the second (and third, and fourth) is where you sculpt it into something great. Being willing to cut, revise, and reshape is what separates a decent story from an unforgettable one.

- When you detach emotionally from specific lines or scenes, you gain clarity on what the story actually needs.

- If something feels out of place, it probably is. Listen to your gut and trust the editing process.
- Many great writers admit their best work comes from cutting and refining, not from adding more.

It's natural to feel attached to our own writing, but true growth as a writer happens when we're willing to let go of our favorite parts if they're not serving the story. The moment you're able to kill your darlings, you free yourself from emotional attachment, allowing you to see your work with fresh eyes. Letting go of something isn't easy, but it's necessary for growth — not just for your writing, but for you as a writer.

TIP 10. THE BEST WRITING APPS YOU DIDN'T KNOW YOU NEEDED

Writing is a craft, but that doesn't mean you have to do everything the hard way. Technology can be a writer's best friend, helping you stay organized, improve clarity, eliminate distractions, and refine your work. Whether you're drafting, editing, or just trying to stay on top of your creative ideas, these underrated writing apps can take your work to the next level.

Here are five must-have writing apps every writer should consider:

1. Scrivener – The Ultimate Manuscript Organizer.

Scrivener is a game-changer for writers working on long-form projects like novels, screenplays, or research-heavy nonfiction. Instead of managing a massive, unwieldy document, Scrivener lets you break your manuscript into sections, move scenes around effortlessly, track character arcs, and store all your notes and research in one place. Whether you're planning or drafting, Scrivener helps keep your thoughts and ideas organized, ensuring your story flows seamlessly from start to finish.

- Best for: Novelists, screenwriters, and researchers.
- Key Features: Virtual index cards, outline view, distraction-free mode, built-in research storage.
- Why You Need It: If you struggle with structuring your story or keeping track of research, Scrivener keeps everything neatly organized and easily accessible.

2. Grammarly – Your Personal AI Editor.

Even the best writers make typos, and that's where Grammarly comes in. More than just a spell-checker, Grammarly analyzes sentence structure, tone, clarity, and engagement, helping you write cleaner, sharper prose. Plus, it gives real-time feedback and suggestions, so you can write confidently knowing your work is polished. It's not just for professionals; it's a game-changer for anyone who wants cleaner, error-free writing!

- Best for: Everyone — from fiction writers to bloggers and business professionals.
- Key Features: Grammar and spell check, clarity suggestions, plagiarism detection, tone analysis.
- Why You Need It: Grammarly helps ensure your writing is polished and professional, catching mistakes before they reach your audience.

3. Hemingway Editor – Make Your Writing Bold and Clear

Inspired by Ernest Hemingway's minimalist style, this tool helps you tighten your prose by highlighting overly complex sentences, passive voice, and excessive adverbs. The goal? To make your writing clear, concise, and punchy. It's like having a personal writing coach that encourages you to simplify your sentences without losing the heart of your message. Great for writers who want their work to be as sharp as possible!

- Best for: Writers who want to improve readability and clarity.
- Key Features: Color-coded feedback, readability score, passive voice detection, adverb alerts.
- Why You Need It: If your writing feels too wordy or clunky, Hemingway Editor will help you refine it for better flow and engagement.

4. Freedom – The App That Blocks Distractions.

Let's be honest, social media, emails, and endless browsing are the biggest enemies of productivity. Freedom lets you block distractions on your phone or computer, helping you stay focused on your writing.

- Best for: Writers who struggle with procrastination.
- Key Features: Customizable block lists, scheduled focus sessions, cross-device syncing.
- Why You Need It: If you find yourself constantly checking your phone or getting lost in internet rabbit holes, Freedom helps you reclaim your focus and stay on track.

5. Evernote – Capture Every Idea Instantly.

Every writer knows the struggle of forgetting a brilliant idea because they didn't write it down in time. Evernote lets you store notes, ideas, and research seamlessly across all your devices, ensuring that inspiration is never lost.

- Best for: Writers who juggle multiple ideas or research-heavy projects.
- Key Features: Cloud syncing, audio note recording, text scanning, organizational tags.
- Why You Need It: Whether you're brainstorming plot ideas, collecting character references, or organizing research, Evernote keeps everything in one place for easy access.

PART 3: STAYING MOTIVATED AND INSPIRED

Staying inspired as a writer requires consistency, creativity, and the ability to push through creative slumps. This section covers key strategies for maintaining motivation, avoiding clichés, using writing prompts for inspiration, applying feedback effectively, and developing compelling characters that keep readers engaged.

TIP 11. HOW TO STAY MOTIVATED WHEN YOU DON'T FEEL LIKE WRITING

We've all been there: staring at a blank page, struggling to find the motivation to write. Whether you're dealing with writer's block, burnout, or just a lack of inspiration, it's hard to get back on track. But don't worry! Here are a few ways to spark your creativity and get yourself writing again:

1. Set Small, Achievable Goals.

When you're feeling unmotivated, it's easy to become overwhelmed by the thought of writing thousands of words. Instead, break your work into bite-sized tasks. Aim for small, specific goals, like writing 500 words, completing a scene, or finishing a paragraph. By hitting these smaller milestones, you'll feel a sense of accomplishment, and that momentum will help you push forward. Even 10 minutes of focused writing can get the ball rolling!

2. Write Every Day, Even if It's Just a Sentence.

Sometimes, the hardest part is starting. Make it a habit to write every day, no matter how little you do. Even if you only manage one sentence, the act of writing consistently keeps the creative muscles strong and ready for when inspiration does strike. It's not about quantity, it's about consistency. Writing a little every day adds up over time, and soon you'll be back in the groove!

3. Remember Why You Started.

When the motivation fades, it helps to reconnect with the passion that first inspired you to write. Was it a story you couldn't wait to tell? A character you needed to bring to life? Reflect on what made you start writing in the first place. Revisit your original goals or dreams and remind yourself of your purpose. Your "why" will reignite that spark and give you the energy to keep going.

TIP 12. WRITING TIP: HOW TO AVOID CLICHÉS IN YOUR WRITING

Clichés are the overused expressions, predictable plotlines, and tired character tropes that can make your writing feel stale and uninspired. While clichés aren't inherently bad, relying on them too much can diminish originality, weaken your storytelling, and make your work feel forgettable. Readers love fresh, unexpected writing that challenges conventions and brings new perspectives to familiar ideas.

To keep your writing engaging and unpredictable, here are three essential ways to break free from clichés and elevate your storytelling.

1. Think Outside the Box with Your Descriptions.

One of the most common places clichés sneak into writing is in descriptions of, emotions, settings, or even actions. Phrases like *"her heart pounded in her chest"* or *"the sun sank below the horizon in a blaze of color"* are so familiar that they fail to evoke strong imagery or emotion anymore.

How to make descriptions more original:

- **Engage all five senses** – Don't just describe what something looks like; incorporate touch, sound, smell, and taste.

  Example: Instead of saying, "The alley smelled bad," try: "The stench of rotting fruit and damp cardboard clung to the air, thick enough to coat the tongue."

- **Avoid generic emotions—show them instead** – Rather than writing *"fear gripped her"*, focus on body language, reactions, and environment to bring fear to life.

  Example: Instead of "She was terrified," try: "Her nails dug into her palms, deep enough to leave half-moon imprints. She swallowed, but the lump in her throat wouldn't budge."

- **Use unexpected comparisons and metaphors** – Instead of **falling back on common similes**, create **fresh, vivid imagery**.

  Example: Instead of "He was as fast as a cheetah," try: "He moved through the crowd like wind through dry leaves—sudden, silent, and gone before anyone noticed."

Examples of great, unique descriptions in literature:

- **Virginia Woolf (*To the Lighthouse*)** – Uses fluid, poetic imagery to describe time, thought, and consciousness.

- **Ray Bradbury (*Fahrenheit 451*)** – Avoids predictable phrases by making descriptions feel almost tactile.

  Example: "The books leapt and danced like roasted birds, their wings ablaze with red and yellow feathers."

- **Toni Morrison (*Beloved*)** – Writes descriptions that feel raw and sensory.

  Example: "There is a loneliness that can be rocked. Arms crossed, knees drawn up; holding, holding on, this motion, unlike a ship's, smooths and contains the rocker."

How to apply this in your writing:

1. Pause before using a common phrase or description and ask if there's a fresher way to say it.
2. Read outside your genre to see how great writers describe emotions and settings differently.
3. Use real-life sensory experiences to craft descriptions that feel authentic and immersive.

2. Create Unique Dialogue that Feels Real.

Dialogue is another area where clichés often sneak in, making conversations feel unnatural, overly dramatic, or too predictable. Readers have seen generic lines like "I have a bad feeling about this" or "You don't have to do this" too many times — they no longer create impact.

How to avoid cliché dialogue:

- **Let characters speak in a way that is unique to them** – A scientist, a teenager, and a detective shouldn't sound the same. Use word choice, sentence structure, and mannerisms that reflect their personality and background.

  Example: Instead of "I will always protect you," a character could say, "Look, I may not be good at much, but keeping you safe? That's the one thing I'll never mess up."

- **Use subtext—don't make everything obvious** – In real life, people rarely say exactly what they mean; emotions often come through in what's left unsaid.

  Example: Instead of "I'm really upset with you," try: "You know, it's funny. I thought you'd be the last person to do something like this."

- **Avoid forced exposition in dialogue** – If characters are just reciting information for the reader's sake, it feels inauthentic.

  Example of forced exposition: "As you know, Sarah, ever since the accident five years ago, you've had trouble trusting people."

  Better version: "It's been five years, and you still flinch every time someone reaches for your hand."

Examples of realistic, powerful dialogue in literature:

- **J. D. Salinger (*The Catcher in the Rye*)** – Captures natural, rambling, and emotional speech that makes Holden Caulfield feel like a real teenager.

- **Aaron Sorkin (*The Social Network*, *The West Wing*)** – Uses sharp, fast-paced dialogue that feels natural and full of subtext.

- **Cormac McCarthy (*No Country for Old Men*)** – His dialogue is minimalist but weighted, making every word feel necessary.

How to apply this in your writing:

1. Read your dialogue aloud. If it sounds forced, unnatural, or robotic, rewrite it.
2. Let characters interrupt, hesitate, and trail off like real people.
3. Cut any dialogue that doesn't serve a purpose. If it doesn't reveal character or advance the plot, remove it.

3. Make Sure Your Characters' Actions Are Unexpected.

Predictable characters who follow familiar arcs can make a story feel like a recycled version of something readers have already seen. If your protagonist always makes the noble choice, or your villain is evil just for the sake of it, your characters might feel one-dimensional and cliché.

How to make characters feel fresh and unpredictable:

- **Challenge stereotypes and tropes** – Instead of using stock character types, flip them on their head.

    Example: Instead of the classic "grizzled, tough detective," create a detective who is soft-spoken, anxiety-ridden, or obsessed with gardening.

- **Give them conflicting motivations** – Real people wrestle with internal contradictions; your characters should too.

    Example: In Breaking Bad, Walter White starts as a sympathetic character, but his greed and pride make him spiral into villainy.

- **Make their decisions feel real, not plot-driven** – Characters shouldn't just make choices because the plot needs them to.

  Example: In The Road, the father's decisions to protect his son feel genuine and heart-wrenching, rather than dictated by cliché heroism.

Examples of unique, dynamic characters in literature:

- **Humbert Humbert (*Lolita*)** – A narrator so charming yet repulsive, readers feel conflicted about him.

- **Lisey Debusher Landon (*Lisey's Story*)** – A widow dealing with grief, trauma, and the surreal, her character is deeply layered.

- **Offred (*The Handmaid's Tale*)** – A protagonist who isn't a warrior or savior, but someone simply trying to survive, making her struggles more personal and impactful.

How to apply this in your writing:

1. Ask: *Does my character's choice surprise me? If not, how can I challenge their decision-making process?*
2. Avoid black-and-white morality. Even heroes should have flaws, and villains should have depth.
3. Make character actions story-driven but deeply personal. They should reflect who they are, not just what the plot needs.

TIP 13. THE POWER OF WRITING PROMPTS

Every writer — whether just starting out or a seasoned novelist — has encountered moments of creative drought. The blank page stares back, ideas feel distant, and the words simply won't come. This is where writing prompts can be a game-changer.

Writing prompts are a creative nudge, designed to spark new ideas, challenge your imagination, and get the words flowing. Think of them as a jumpstart for your creativity, helping you break free from writer's block and explore new territories in your storytelling.

Let's dive into how writing prompts can transform your writing process and elevate your craft.

1. They Spark New Ideas.

Sometimes, the hardest part of writing isn't the actual writing, it's coming up with an idea worth exploring. Writing prompts act like a creative spark, igniting fresh concepts that you might never have considered on your own.

How writing prompts help generate ideas:

- **They introduce new scenarios** – A prompt might suggest, "A letter arrives in the mail, with no return address, and inside is a single key." This simple idea can lead to a mystery, a love story, or even a horror novel—depending on how you interpret it.

- **They force your brain to make new connections** – Sometimes, you just need a starting point to unlock a wave of creativity. A random phrase like "Write a story about a world where people can erase memories like deleting files on a computer" might inspire an entire novel.

- **They remove the pressure of originality** – Often, writers get stuck because they feel they need a groundbreaking idea. But with prompts, you're free to experiment without the weight of needing it to be "perfect."

Examples of great prompts to spark ideas:

- *"Your character wakes up in a parallel universe where everything is exactly the same, except one detail that changes everything."*

- *"Write about a conversation between two strangers at an airport who realize they have an unexpected connection."*

- *"A famous painting in a museum goes missing, but no one remembers it ever existed, except your protagonist."*

How to apply this in your writing:

1. Pick a random prompt and write freely for 10–15 minutes without overthinking.
2. Try using a writing prompt generator (such as Reedsy, Writer's Digest, or The Story Shack) for unexpected ideas.
3. Combine multiple prompts — take a character from one, a setting from another, and mix them into something unique.

Remember: The goal isn't to create a masterpiece right away. It's to get the creative gears turning.

2. They Push You Out of Your Comfort Zone.

We all have favorite genres, styles, and themes we tend to gravitate toward. Writing prompts can force you to break out of those patterns and explore ideas you wouldn't normally tackle.

How writing prompts encourage creative growth:

- **They introduce new perspectives** – A prompt like "Tell a story from the perspective of an inanimate object" forces you to think differently. What would a clock, a tree, or a forgotten diary have to say?

- **They help you experiment with different genres** – If you always write romance, try a prompt in horror or sci-fi. If you love contemporary fiction, explore fantasy. Example: "Your character wakes up one morning to find they've switched bodies with someone on the other side of the world." This could be a thriller, a comedy, or a heartfelt drama, depending on how you approach it.

- **They develop new writing skills** – A great writer is a versatile one. Prompts challenge you to write in first person when you're used to third, or focus on atmosphere when you typically prioritize dialogue.

How to step outside your comfort zone with prompts:

1. Pick a genre you rarely write in and use a prompt to craft a short story.
2. Challenge yourself to write from an unusual perspective (a villain, an unreliable narrator, an alien seeing Earth for the first time).

3. Set a word count limit—try writing a 200-word flash fiction piece based on a prompt to develop concise storytelling skills.

Tip: Some of the best ideas come when you venture into the unknown — writing prompts help you stretch beyond your creative limits.

3. They Get You Writing When You Feel Stuck.

Writer's block can feel paralyzing but the best way to overcome it is simply to write anything, even if it's messy. Writing prompts take the pressure off because they give you something to respond to, rather than waiting for inspiration to magically strike.

How prompts help break creative paralysis:

- **They remove the fear of a blank page** – Instead of staring at an empty document, you have a concrete idea to build from.

- **They create momentum** – Once you start writing—even if it's just a small response to a prompt—your brain begins generating new connections and possibilities.

- **They can lead to unexpected breakthroughs** – What starts as a simple prompt exercise could evolve into a novel-worthy idea.

Examples of prompts for breaking writer's block:

- "Write a letter that your main character never sends."

- "Describe your childhood home using only sounds and smells."

- "Write a scene where two characters meet for the first time—but one of them already knows the other's darkest secret."

How to use prompts when you're stuck:

1. Choose a low-pressure prompt and free-write without judgment or editing for five minutes.
2. Set a goal to write one short piece using a prompt every day for a week.
3. Take a character from your current work-in-progress and place them in a completely different situation using a random prompt. This can help develop their personality.

The key is to start—once the words are flowing, ideas will follow.

TIP 14. HOW TO USE FEEDBACK TO IMPROVE YOUR WRITING

Receiving feedback on your writing can be one of the most valuable, yet intimidating experiences in your creative journey. It's never easy to hear that something isn't quite working—but learning to embrace critique and use it to your advantage is what separates a good writer from a great one.

The truth is, even the most successful authors rely on feedback to refine their work. Every novel, screenplay, or poem you love has been through multiple rounds of critique and revision before it became the polished version you see today. So, instead of fearing feedback, think of it as a roadmap to making your story stronger.

Here's how to approach feedback with the right mindset and use it to take your writing to the next level.

1. Stay Open to Constructive Criticism.

Let's be real, criticism is tough. When someone points out flaws in your story, it's natural to feel a knee-jerk reaction of frustration, doubt, or even defensiveness. But constructive criticism isn't meant to tear you down, it's meant to build you up by showing you areas where your writing can improve.

How to embrace constructive feedback effectively:

- **Detach from your work emotionally** – Your story is personal, but remember that critiques are about the writing, not about you as a writer.

- **Look for patterns** – If multiple people mention the same issue (e.g., "the pacing feels slow," or "the main character lacks depth"), that's a sign it needs attention.

- **Ask clarifying questions** – If feedback is vague, don't be afraid to ask for specifics. For example, if someone says "this scene doesn't work," ask why? Is it the dialogue? The pacing? The stakes?

Examples of famous writers who embraced feedback:

- **Stephen King (*On Writing*)** – Describes how his wife's brutal yet honest feedback on *Carrie* helped him cut unnecessary fluff and sharpen the story.

- **J. K. Rowling** – *Harry Potter and the Sorcerer's Stone* was rejected 12 times, but she took feedback, revised, and persisted until it became a worldwide phenomenon.

- **Ernest Hemingway** – Famously rewrote the ending of *A Farewell to Arms* 39 times before he was satisfied with it.

How to apply this in your writing:

1. When you receive feedback, sit with it for a day or two before reacting.
2. Highlight areas where multiple critiques overlap because those are your biggest opportunities for improvement.
3. Instead of seeing criticism as a setback, see it as a chance to refine your work and grow as a writer.

2. Don't Take It Personally.

Writing is an intensely personal process. You pour time, effort, and heart into every sentence, so when someone suggests a change, it can feel like they're questioning your talent. But the truth is, feedback is about the story, not about you as a person.

How to separate yourself from the critique:

- **Remind yourself that every great writer has faced criticism.** Even literary legends like Jane Austen, F. Scott Fitzgerald, and Agatha Christie had editors who told them to make changes.

- **Understand that feedback is a sign of engagement.** If someone is critiquing your work, it means they cared enough to give it thoughtful attention. That's a good thing!

- **Recognize the difference between constructive and unhelpful criticism.** Constructive feedback is specific and aimed at improving the story (e.g., "The antagonist's motivation feels weak — consider giving them a personal stake in the conflict"). Unhelpful feedback is vague, harsh, or dismissive (e.g., "I just didn't like this"). Focus on the former, and ignore the latter.

Famous examples of writers overcoming harsh criticism:

- Stephen King threw the first draft of *Carrie* in the trash because he thought it wasn't good enough—his wife rescued it, gave him feedback, and convinced him to keep going.

- William Golding's *Lord of the Flies* was rejected 21 times before finding a publisher — imagine if he had given up!

- Margaret Mitchell's *Gone with the Wind* was rejected 38 times, but after revisions, it became one of the most successful novels of all time.

How to apply this in your writing:

1. Instead of seeing feedback as a personal attack, view it as a chance to learn and refine your craft.
2. If a critique stings, take a break before responding. Time helps you see feedback more objectively.
3. Separate ego from improvement. The best writers never stop learning.

3. Use Feedback to Improve Your Work, not Change Your Voice.

Not all feedback is worth following. While critiques can help strengthen your story, it's important to stay true to your vision and unique writing style. The goal is to enhance your work, not strip away what makes it special.

How to know which feedback to take and which to ignore:

- **Does the feedback improve clarity, pacing, or character development?** If yes, it's worth considering.

- **Is the critique about personal preference rather than actual issues?** If someone says, *"I don't like first-person narratives"* but your story is written in first-person, that's their opinion, not a problem with your writing.

- **Are multiple people pointing out the same issue?** If yes, it's likely something worth fixing.

Examples of writers who stuck to their voice despite criticism:

- **Toni Morrison (*Beloved*)** – Faced criticism for her complex narratives but stayed true to her lyrical, multi-layered storytelling.

- **George Orwell (*1984*)** – Editors pushed him to soften his bleak dystopian vision, but he refused, resulting in one of the most impactful novels ever written.

- **Harper Lee (*To Kill a Mockingbird*)** – Was originally advised to scrap parts of the novel, but she stuck to her vision, creating a timeless classic.

How to apply this in your writing:

1. Trust your instincts. If a suggestion feels right, incorporate it. If it doesn't, set it aside.
2. Stay open to changes that strengthen the story, but don't compromise your unique voice.

3. Ask yourself: *Does this feedback align with the kind of writer I want to be?* If yes, use it. If not, thank the person and move on.

TIP 15. HOW TO DEVELOP STRONG CHARACTERS THAT READERS WILL LOVE

Characters are the beating heart of any great story. They're the reason readers laugh, cry, and stay up late turning pages. A well-written plot may draw people in, but it's the characters that make them care, the ones they root for, agonize over, and sometimes even see themselves in.

Think about the most memorable characters in literature, film, and television. They aren't just interesting because of what they do; they resonate because of who they are. From Elizabeth Bennet (*Pride and Prejudice*) to Jay Gatsby (*The Great Gatsby*) to Atticus Finch (*To Kill a Mockingbird*), what makes them so unforgettable? They feel real, layered, and deeply human.

If you want to create characters that readers will love (or love to hate), here's how to bring them to life on the page.

1. Give Them Clear Motivations.

Every great character has a reason for doing what they do. Their motivations drive their actions, decisions, and reactions throughout the story. Whether it's a desire for love, revenge, freedom, or personal growth, knowing what pushes your character forward gives them purpose and makes them feel real. Ask yourself: What does my character want most? What are they willing to sacrifice to get it? When your character's motivations are clear, readers will understand why they make certain choices and will be invested in seeing them succeed (or fail).

How to craft strong motivations:

- Make their **goal personal** — it's not just about saving the world, it's about protecting a specific person, fulfilling a dream, or proving something to themselves.

- Let them **face moral dilemmas** — what will they sacrifice to achieve their goal?

- Ensure their motivation **stays consistent** but can evolve as the story progresses.

Examples of powerful character motivations:

- **Jayber Crow (Jayber Crow by Wendell Berry)** – A barber in a small town, Jayber wrestles with his place in the world, the meaning of love, and his unspoken devotion to a woman he can never have, making his quiet longing deeply compelling.

- **Humbert Humbert (Lolita by Vladimir Nabokov)** – Though despicable, his motivation—his obsession and twisted love—is so meticulously explored that readers are pulled into his deeply unreliable mind.

- **Rick Blaine (Casablanca)** – His jaded, self-serving nature is challenged by love and duty, forcing him to choose between personal happiness and a cause greater than himself.

How to apply this in your writing:

1. Ask: What does my character want more than anything?
2. How does this drive their decisions, relationships, and mistakes?
3. If their motivation changes, what causes that shift?

2. Show Their Flaws and Strengths.

No one is perfect, and neither should your characters be! To make them feel real and relatable, give them a balance of both strengths and flaws. Perhaps your protagonist is brave but too impulsive, or maybe they're compassionate but struggle with self-doubt. These imperfections make characters more multidimensional and human. It's through their weaknesses that readers connect with them, while their strengths inspire admiration. The key is to create well-rounded characters who feel like people we know.

How to balance strengths and weaknesses:

- **Give your character an ability or trait that sets them apart, but pair it with a weakness that complicates their journey.**

Example: A brilliant scientist whose obsession with perfection alienates the people they love.

- **Let them fail.** Failure makes a character's ultimate victory meaningful.

Example: A warrior who hesitates at the wrong moment, costing them something irreparable.

- **Show how their greatest strength is also a weakness.**

Example: A charismatic leader whose ability to inspire others leads them into dangerous territory, where they are blinded by their own vision.

Examples of flawed, complex characters:

- **Florence Green (The Bookshop by Penelope Fitzgerald)** – A woman trying to open a bookshop in a small town, her resilience is both her strength and her downfall, as she underestimates the town's quiet hostility.

- **Randle McMurphy (One Flew Over the Cuckoo's Nest by Ken Kesey)** – Charismatic and rebellious, his defiance makes him a hero, but also leads to his ultimate destruction.

- **Michael Corleone (The Godfather, film adaptation)** – He begins as a reluctant leader, but his transformation into a ruthless crime boss turns his initial strength — loyalty — into his greatest downfall.

How to apply this in your writing:

1. What flaws make your character's journey harder?
2. Does their strength ever lead them to make the wrong choice?
3. How does their flaw set up a moment of crisis or growth later in the story?

3. Let Them Evolve Throughout the Story.

One of the most compelling aspects of storytelling is watching characters grow and change. Over the course of your story, allow your characters to learn from their mistakes, overcome obstacles, and develop new perspectives. Whether they become stronger, wiser, or more vulnerable, their evolution will keep readers engaged and invested in their journey. A static character may feel flat, but a character who evolves feels dynamic and real. Transformation is the heartbeat of character-driven narratives.

How to create a strong character arc:

- **Start them in one place but end them somewhere different.** What lessons do they learn? What do they lose?

- **Make the change gradual and believable.** Real transformation happens slowly, through challenges and setbacks.

- **Tie their growth to the themes of the story.** How does their arc reflect the bigger message?

Examples of unforgettable character arcs:

- **Hester Prynne (The Scarlet Letter by Nathaniel Hawthorne)** – Cast out for her sin, Hester transforms from a symbol of shame to one of quiet resilience and strength, changing the perception of both herself and those around her.

- **Paul Edgecomb (The Green Mile by Stephen King)** – The prison guard who witnesses supernatural miracles and human cruelty ultimately learns that justice is not always black and white, leaving him a changed man.

- **Sal Paradise (On the Road by Jack Kerouac)** – His journey of freedom and self-discovery leads him to a realization about the fleeting nature of experience and connection, forcing him to confront what he truly seeks.

How to apply this in your writing:

1. What lessons does your character need to learn?
2. How do the events of the story force them to change?
3. Does their journey end in triumph, tragedy, or ambiguity?

PART 4: MASTERING STORYTELLING TECHNIQUES

Great storytelling isn't just about having a compelling plot, it's about how you bring it to life on the page. This chapter explores how to write natural, engaging dialogue, create gripping scenes that keep readers hooked, and build tension that drives the story forward.

TIP 16. THE IMPORTANCE OF DIALOGUE IN STORYTELLING

Dialogue is more than just words exchanged between characters — it's the heartbeat of a story, shaping relationships, building tension, and immersing readers in the world of the narrative. Great dialogue has the power to transform a story, making it feel authentic, dynamic, and emotionally charged.

Think of some of the most unforgettable moments in literature and film. Often, they aren't just action sequences or dramatic monologues, but sharp, revealing conversations. From the witty, fast-paced exchanges in *The West Wing* to the icy confrontations in *No Country for Old Men*, dialogue is where characters reveal their true selves.

Whether it's a quiet, vulnerable confession or a tense standoff filled with subtext, dialogue is one of the most powerful tools a writer has. Here's why it's so essential:

1. It Reveals Personality.

Dialogue is one of the best ways to show who your characters truly are. The way they speak, whether it's casual, formal, sarcastic, or poetic, reveals their background, values, and emotions. For example, a character who uses humor to deflect serious conversations may be hiding insecurities, while one who speaks with purpose and clarity could show strong leadership. Pay attention to how your characters talk. Do they use slang, or do they speak with precision? Do they interrupt others, or are they more reserved? The nuances of their speech can reveal as much about them as their actions.

How to use dialogue to reveal character:

- **A reserved, calculating character** might speak in short, clipped sentences, giving nothing away.

Example: In The Silence of the Lambs, Dr. Hannibal Lecter's precise, articulate speech contrasts with his monstrous nature, making him even more unsettling.

- **A character who rambles or talks in metaphors** may be thoughtful but scattered, showing a creative mind at work.

Example: In Alice's Adventures in Wonderland, the Mad Hatter's eccentric, nonsensical dialogue reflects the absurdity of Wonderland.

- **A tough, no-nonsense character** might use direct, simple speech, avoiding unnecessary words.

Example: Raymond Chandler's hard-boiled detective, Philip Marlowe, speaks in sharp, witty one-liners that define him as a man who's always in control, even when everything is falling apart.

- **Characters from different social classes, regions, or time periods** will speak differently.

Example: In A Streetcar Named Desire, Blanche DuBois' refined, poetic speech contrasts with Stanley Kowalski's blunt, working-class dialogue, highlighting their deep incompatibility.

How to apply this in your writing:

1. Listen to real conversations. People speak in unique rhythms, with hesitations, quirks, and interruptions.
2. Consider your character's background. Education, culture, personality, and past experiences all shape how they speak.
3. Read dialogue out loud. If it sounds unnatural, rewrite it.

2. It Moves the Plot Forward.

Dialogue isn't just for character development; it's also a crucial storytelling tool. Well-crafted conversations can convey information, create conflict, and push the plot ahead. Instead of summarizing events or thoughts in a narrative, you can have characters discuss key plot points or make important decisions through their dialogue. For instance, a simple exchange like "We need to get out of here before they come back" creates urgency and drives the action forward. Effective dialogue gives the story momentum and ensures that every conversation counts in the larger narrative.

How to use dialogue to move the plot forward:

- Instead of **telling** the reader information, reveal it through conversation.

Example: In The Great Escape, the prisoners don't simply narrate their escape plan to the reader — instead, they strategize and debate in hushed conversations, creating a sense of urgency.

- Use **subtext**! Let characters say one thing while meaning another.

Example: In Gone with the Wind, Rhett Butler's famous line, "Frankly, my dear, I don't give a damn," isn't just a farewell — it's the culmination of years of toxic love and unfulfilled longing.

- Create **questions that demand answers**—dialogue should make the reader want to know what happens next.

Example: In The Godfather, Michael Corleone's chilling words — "I'll make him an offer he can't refuse" — set the stage for the power and violence that will follow.

How to apply this in your writing:

1. Trim unnecessary exchanges. Skip greetings, small talk, and filler words that don't serve a purpose.
2. Make every line count. Does this dialogue reveal something new, deepen the tension, or move the plot forward?
3. Use dialogue-driven scenes for pacing. Fast, sharp dialogue speeds things up, while slower, reflective conversations let readers breathe.

3. It Creates Tension and Drama.

The right dialogue can intensify the emotional stakes in your story. Whether it's a heated argument, a quiet moment of revelation, or a flirtatious exchange, dialogue adds layers of tension and drama. It's the tool through which characters clash, reveal secrets, or express desire. When characters with opposing goals or viewpoints interact, dialogue can become a battleground for power. Think of any great conflict in literature, often, it's the words spoken in those moments that truly drive the emotional impact home. Words have power, and when used effectively, they can keep readers on the edge of their seats.

How to create tension with dialogue:

- **Two characters with opposing goals** create instant conflict.

Example: In 12 Angry Men, an entire jury room is filled with opposing opinions, and the story's intensity builds through sharp, escalating dialogue.

- **The things left unsaid are just as important as what's spoken.**

Example: In No Country for Old Men, the terrifying gas station scene between Anton Chigurh and the clerk is filled with subtext and unspoken menace, as Chigurh plays a deadly game over a coin flip.

- **Interruptions, pauses, and miscommunication create drama.**

Example: In A Streetcar Named Desire, Stanley Kowalski's rough, aggressive speech constantly interrupts and overpowers Blanche's refined, fragile dialogue, showing his dominance in their toxic relationship.

Examples of dialogue-driven tension:

- **Tennessee Williams'** *A Streetcar Named Desire* – Conversations drip with underlying violence, sexual tension, and emotional instability, keeping readers on edge.

- **Quentin Tarantino's** *Inglourious Basterds* – The opening farmhouse scene is a masterclass in suspense, where polite conversation slowly transforms into psychological warfare.

- **Harper Lee's** *To Kill a Mockingbird* – Atticus Finch's courtroom speech is both a moment of persuasion and dramatic intensity, exposing racial injustice while revealing the biases of the townspeople.

How to apply this in your writing:

1. Don't spell everything out. Let the reader pick up on tension through subtext.
2. Use interruptions and silences. A well-placed pause can say more than a full sentence.
3. Make dialogue feel like a battle. When characters want different things, their words become weapons.

TIP 17. HOW TO WRITE A SCENE THAT KEEPS YOUR READERS HOOKED

Want to keep your readers on edge, unable to put your book down? Writing a gripping scene isn't just about fast-paced action, it's about momentum, tension, and leaving the audience hungry for more. Every scene in your story should serve a purpose, whether it's advancing the plot, revealing character depth, or escalating conflict.

Think about the most memorable scenes you've read, ones that made you turn the page without hesitation. Maybe it was the eerie, quiet buildup before a monster attack in Stephen King's *It*, or the razor-sharp dialogue exchanges in Gillian Flynn's *Gone Girl*, or even the high-stakes duels in George R. R. Martin's *A Song of Ice and Fire* series.

So, what makes a scene truly gripping? Let's break it down into three essential techniques that will make your writing impossible to ignore.

1. Start with Action.

The best scenes grab your reader's attention right from the first sentence. Begin with something immediate, a burst of action, a sudden event, or a high-stakes situation that throws the character (and the reader) right into the heart of the scene. This doesn't mean you have to start with a physical fight or explosion, but you should be thinking about how you can immerse the reader instantly.

An exciting action can be:

1. A heated argument that reveals secrets.
2. A mysterious knock at the door in the middle of the night.
3. A character running late for an important event — only to find disaster waiting.
4. A sudden realization that changes everything.

Examples of strong opening action in scenes:

- *"The door burst open, and two men came crashing through, their eyes wild and their breath labored."* (*The Girl with the Dragon Tattoo* – Stieg Larsson)

- *"We should have never gone to the basement."* (*Lock Every Door* – Riley Sager)

- *"The night Max wore his wolf suit and made mischief of one kind and another, his mother called him 'WILD THING! And Max said, I'LL EAT YOU UP!'"* (*Where the Wild Things Are* – Maurice Sendak)

How to apply this:

1. Open your scene in the middle of an event rather than leading up to it.
2. Use strong, active verbs to create immediacy (e.g., *She slammed the door* vs. *She closed the door*).
3. Keep the opening short, punchy, and filled with movement.

2. Raise the Stakes.

Once the action begins, keep the pressure mounting. Every scene should have something at stake — whether it's a personal goal, a physical threat, or emotional turmoil. Increase the tension by making the situation progressively harder for your character to overcome. Maybe they have less time to make a crucial decision, or they realize they've made a mistake that might cost them dearly.

Stakes can be:

- **Physical:** A detective chasing a suspect through dark alleyways.
- **Emotional:** A woman debating whether to read a letter that could destroy her marriage.
- **Moral:** A character forced to choose between betraying a friend or losing everything.

Examples of how stakes build in a scene:

- In J. K. Rowling's Harry Potter and the Sorcerer's Stone, the moment Harry and his friends play Wizard's Chess is intense because the pieces physically attack them — losing means more than just failing a game.*

- In The Hunger Games by Suzanne Collins, every fight Katniss enters isn't just about survival — it's about defying the oppressive system that put her there.

- In Rebecca by Daphne du Maurier, the narrator constantly faces the threat of being discovered as an imposter, even though no one outright suspects her.

How to apply this:

1. Ask: *What's the worst thing that could happen right now?* Then, push your characters toward it.
2. Keep upping the tension — just when things seem stable, throw in a twist.
3. Introduce time pressure or constraints (e.g., a bomb about to go off, a deadline approaching)

3. End with a Cliffhanger or Question.

Don't let your reader off the hook too easily, end the scene with a cliffhanger, a dramatic twist, or an unresolved question that leaves them craving more. Whether it's a character about to make a life-changing choice, a new mystery uncovered, or a shocking revelation, closing with a sense of uncertainty compels readers to keep turning the pages. A well-placed cliffhanger or open-ended moment ensures that readers can't help but move on to the next scene.

A cliffhanger can be:

- A sudden interruption (a gunshot rings out, the lights go off).
- A mystery deepening (a character finds an unsigned letter with shocking information).
- A twist revelation (the person they thought was dead... isn't).
- An emotional bombshell (someone confesses a deep secret, but the response is left unread).

Examples of gripping scene endings:

- *"And then he was gone."* (*The Road* – Cormac McCarthy)
- *"He opened the letter, his hands shaking. Inside was a single sentence that changed everything."*
- *"She turned around to run — but it was too late."*

How to apply this:

1. End mid-action or right before a crucial moment (make readers desperate to turn the page!).
2. Ask: *What question is left unanswered in this scene?*
3. Keep the resolution just out of reach, so the reader has to keep going.

Just remember that a great scene doesn't just happen, it's crafted with purpose. Whether it's a dramatic confrontation, a shocking revelation, or a quiet moment filled with tension, each scene should add momentum to the story.

To keep readers hooked, remember to:

1. Start in the middle of the action — no long lead-ups.
2. Raise the stakes — keep your characters in tough situations.

3. End with a cliffhanger, question, or unresolved tension — make readers NEED to continue.

TIP 18. HOW TO CREATE TENSION IN YOUR WRITING

Tension is the heartbeat of a compelling story. It's the force that keeps readers turning pages late into the night, breathless to find out what happens next. Whether it's the suspense of an impending disaster, the emotional strain of a fractured relationship, or the quiet intensity of an unsaid truth, tension is what drives a story forward.

Think about some of the most unforgettable books or movies you've encountered. Whether it's the nail-biting anxiety of *Gone Girl* by Gillian Flynn, the quiet dread in Shirley Jackson's *We Have Always Lived in the Castle*, or the relentless suspense of *Jurassic Park* by Michael Crichton, these stories masterfully manipulate tension to keep readers completely absorbed.

So, how do you create that sense of gripping uncertainty in your own writing? Here are three powerful techniques:

1. Give Characters Conflicting Goals.

The more your characters want different things, the more tension you create between them. Conflicting goals drive conflict and create a push-pull dynamic that makes scenes engaging. For example, a character might want to protect a loved one while another wants to reveal a dangerous secret, and both desires can't coexist without consequences. This conflict can be internal (a character torn between love and duty) or external (two characters fighting for the same goal). When characters' motivations clash, the stakes grow higher, and the reader is left wondering how it will all resolve. The constant back-and-forth keeps tension at a high level.

Examples of conflicting goals creating tension:

- In The Great Gatsby, Gatsby wants to recreate the past and win back Daisy, but Daisy is torn between her love for Gatsby and her comfortable, established life with Tom. Their opposing desires create emotional tension that drives the story forward.

- In Lord of the Rings, Frodo's goal is to destroy the One Ring, while Gollum desperately wants to reclaim it. Their uneasy alliance creates constant tension, as Gollum teeters between helping and betraying Frodo at every turn.

- In Breaking Bad, Walter White wants to provide for his family through crime, while his brother-in-law, a DEA agent, wants to take down drug operations — unknowingly targeting Walt.

How to apply this:

1. Ask: *What does my protagonist want?* Now, make sure another character wants the exact opposite.
2. Make goals mutually exclusive. If one character succeeds, another must fail.
3. Create internal vs. external conflict: a character might be at war with themselves while also facing external opposition.

2. Make the Stakes High!

There's no tension without something to lose. High stakes are crucial for creating urgency and making readers emotionally invested in the outcome. Whether it's a life-and-death situation, a relationship on the brink of breaking, or a race against time, the higher the stakes, the more tension you'll generate. Think about the last thriller or emotional drama you read, chances are, you were hooked because you could sense that everything was on the line. You need to make your readers feel that same sense of urgency by showing them exactly what's at risk. The fear of losing something important - whether it's love, freedom, or safety - keeps readers engaged and wanting to know what happens next.

Stakes could be:

- A relationship on the verge of collapse.
- A long-held secret that, if exposed, could ruin a life.
- A competition where losing means more than just defeat — the characters loss of self, or public humiliation.

Examples of high stakes in action:

- In *The Handmaid's Tale*, Offred's stake is her freedom — every move she makes could mean life or death.

- In *Pride and Prejudice*, Elizabeth's stake is personal happiness vs. societal expectation — if she marries for security, she risks losing love.

- In *A Quiet Place*, the stakes couldn't be higher — if the characters make a single sound, they die.

How to apply this:

1. Ask: *What is my character's worst fear? Now, put them in a situation where they risk exactly that.*

2. Give your character something so valuable that losing it would destroy them emotionally, physically, or morally.
3. Show the consequences of failure — what will happen if they don't succeed?

3. Use Suspenseful Pacing.

Pacing is a powerful tool for creating tension. By controlling the flow of information, you can keep readers on edge. For example, drag out a crucial moment by describing the environment, the character's reactions, and building up to the climax, while leaving out key details until just the right moment. Slow pacing at key points creates anticipation, making readers impatient and anxious for the resolution. Alternatively, fast pacing during moments of high tension can increase the feeling of urgency, making readers feel like they're racing to the end with the characters. Balancing these pacing techniques creates a rhythmic push and pull that keeps tension high and your readers hooked.

Two key pacing techniques:

- **Slow Down Tension** – When a moment is suspenseful, slow the pacing down to drag out the anxiety. Describe minute details, character reactions, and small, unsettling elements.
    - **Example:** A character creeping through a dark house, every floorboard creaking beneath their feet, heart pounding, shadows shifting…

- **Speed Up Urgency** – During high-stakes moments, shorten sentences, cut unnecessary details, and increase intensity.

- o **Example:** A chase scene where every second counts — brief, sharp sentences mirror the adrenaline of the moment.

Examples of pacing used for tension:

- In The Shining, Stephen King uses long, drawn-out descriptions to build suspense before Jack Torrance's outbursts, making the reader feel the tension before it explodes.

- In The Da Vinci Code, Dan Brown uses short, rapid chapters and quick pacing to make each moment feel urgent and thrilling.

How to apply this:

1. During tense moments, describe small details (shaky hands, flickering lights, a ticking clock).
2. Leave out key information until just the right moment (build anticipation).
3. In high-intensity moments, cut long descriptions, shorten sentences, and move quickly.

Creating tension is about making the reader feel the stakes, uncertainty, and urgency in every scene. The best tension keeps readers nervous, excited, and desperate to turn the page.

TIP 19. THE BENEFITS OF WRITING EVERY DAY (EVEN JUST FOR 10 MINUTES)

If you want to improve as a writer, the key isn't just about writing longer hours, it's about making writing a daily habit. Even if you only write for 10 minutes a day, the benefits are huge. Here's how committing to writing every day, even in small chunks, can transform your writing:

1. Improve Your Skills.

Writing regularly gives you the opportunity to practice your craft and fine-tune your skills. Just like any other skill, writing improves with consistent practice. When you write daily, you begin to notice patterns in your writing, develop your voice, and refine your technique. You might stumble upon new ways to express yourself, discover more about your characters, or get more comfortable with different writing styles. Even short, focused writing sessions can lead to significant improvements over time, as you develop fluency and confidence in your writing.

2. Help You Build Consistency.

Consistency is the backbone of any successful writing career. When you write every day, even for a short period, you begin to build a habit that becomes ingrained in your routine. It's not about writing a masterpiece every day but about making writing a part of your life. The more consistent you are, the easier it becomes to keep going. Writing regularly means you won't fall into long gaps of inactivity. Instead, you'll keep momentum going, and before you know it, those 10-minute sessions will add up to pages, chapters, and full manuscripts.

3. Keep Your Creative Juices Flowing.

Writing every day keeps your creativity flowing and your imagination engaged. When you take a break from writing, it's easy for your ideas to start feeling stale or blocked. But daily writing helps prevent that creative dry spell. Even if you feel uninspired, forcing yourself to write for just a few minutes can spark new ideas, bring clarity to your existing work, or get you excited about an unexpected direction in your story. It's about showing up for your creativity, even when you don't feel like it. The more you write, the more ideas you'll generate, and the more momentum you'll build.

TIP 20. THE BEST TIME TO WRITE: MORNING, NOON, OR NIGHT?

When's the best time to write? This is a question every writer asks themselves at some point, and the truth is, there's no one-size-fits-all answer. Here's a breakdown of the most common writing times:

1. Morning.

For some writers, mornings are magical. The world is still quiet, distractions are minimal, and there's a sense of freshness and possibility in the air. Many writers swear by the early hours of the day, when their minds are clear and they haven't yet been bogged down by the events of the day. If you're someone who wakes up early, enjoys a cup of coffee, and jumps straight into writing, morning might be your sweet spot. The stillness of the morning can help you focus deeply and work uninterrupted.

2. Afternoon.

Others find their stride in the afternoon, when the day's rhythm is already in full swing. For me personally, I love writing during the quiet afternoon hours. There's something about that post-lunch lull when the ideas start to flow freely. By this time, I've had my morning coffee, caught up on emails, and my brain is awake enough to dive deep into creative work without feeling fatigued. If you're not a morning person, the afternoon might be the perfect window to unleash your creativity.

3. Night.

And then, there are those who thrive when the sun sets. Late-night writing is a favorite for many because it's when the world quiets down and distractions fade. For night owls, this time feels like their zone, because their mind lets go of the day's stresses and creativity seems to pour out effortlessly. If you're someone who gets a burst of energy after dinner or enjoys the peace of writing under the moonlight, you might be a night writer.

So, what's the best time to write? It's different for everyone, and that's the beauty of it. It's about finding when your mind is most alert, your ideas are flowing, and you can dive into your story with focus and passion.

PART 5: FINDING BALANCE AS A WRITER

Writing isn't just about the craft. It's about managing your time, energy, and well-being. This section explores how to balance writing with a busy life, maintain discipline without burnout, and incorporate writing into daily routines.

TIP 21. HOW TO BALANCE WRITING WITH A BUSY LIFE

Balancing writing with a busy life can feel like a juggling act but trust me, it's possible! Writing doesn't have to be an all-or-nothing endeavour, and there are ways to incorporate it into your day without feeling overwhelmed. Here's how to manage your writing, even when life gets hectic:

1. Set Realistic Writing Goals.

It's easy to get discouraged when your writing goals feel too big, especially with a packed schedule. That's why it's important to set goals that are achievable, even if you only have a limited amount of time. Instead of aiming to write a whole chapter or 3,000 words, focus on smaller, more manageable targets. Maybe it's writing for 20 minutes a day, or completing a paragraph or two. These smaller wins add up over time, and they prevent burnout. By setting realistic goals, you can stay on track and feel accomplished without adding pressure to your already full life.

2. Write in Short Bursts when You Can.

Life is busy, and finding long stretches of time to write can be tough. But the good news is you don't need hours to be productive. Writing in short bursts can be just as effective. Whether it's during a lunch break, in between meetings, or while waiting for dinner to cook, try squeezing in 10-20 minute writing sessions. These mini-writing sprints are great for focusing on a specific task, whether it's drafting a scene or brainstorming ideas. Over time, these short bursts add up and can lead to significant progress without eating into the rest of your day.

3. Prioritize Writing like Any Other Job.

One of the best ways to balance writing with a busy life is to treat it with the same importance as any other work or responsibility. Put it on your calendar. Set aside dedicated time for writing, just like you would for a meeting or an appointment. Even if it's just 30 minutes a day, having a set writing time makes it easier to stay consistent. If you treat writing as a priority, it becomes a non-negotiable part of your routine, and that makes it easier to manage.

TIP 22. THE POWER OF A WRITING ROUTINE

A writing routine can truly transform the way you approach your craft and boost your productivity! Whether you're working on a novel, a blog post, or a short story, having a set routine can make a world of difference. Here's why:

1. It Trains Your Brain to Focus During Set Times.

One of the key benefits of a writing routine is that it trains your brain to focus during specific time blocks. When you set a designated writing time every day, your mind starts to recognize it as *writing time* - no distractions, no procrastination. It's like creating a mental cue. This conditioning helps you tune out external noise and concentrate more deeply, allowing you to work more efficiently and effectively. The more you stick to your routine, the more your brain gets in the habit of switching into "writing mode" when it's time to write.

2. It Creates Consistency and Discipline.

Consistency is the key to progress in writing. A routine brings structure to your day and makes it easier to sit down and write, even when you're not feeling inspired. It also cultivates discipline, as you're committing to writing on a regular basis, whether you feel like it or not. Even on days when motivation is low, the habit of showing up and sticking to your routine keeps you moving forward. Over time, this consistent effort adds up to significant progress on your projects.

3. It Helps You Make Writing a Habit, not a Chore.

When writing becomes a regular part of your day, it stops feeling like a task or a burden. A writing routine turns writing into a habit, something you do naturally rather than forcing yourself to do. Instead of viewing it as an obligation, you start to look forward to it as a creative outlet or an essential part of your routine, just like eating or exercising. Over time, this shift in perspective makes writing feel less like work and more like something you enjoy and prioritize.

Having a writing routine isn't about forcing yourself to write for hours each day, it's about creating a sustainable habit that fits into your life. Whether it's 15 minutes every morning or a couple of hours every evening, a routine that works for you will help you build momentum and make writing a consistent, enjoyable part of your life.

TIP 23. WRITING WITH EMOTION: HOW TO MAKE YOUR READERS FEEL SOMETHING

Emotion is the core of every unforgettable story. No matter how intricate your plot or how imaginative your setting, it's the emotions that linger in a reader's mind long after they turn the last page. Readers may not remember every event, but they'll remember how a story made them feel.

Think about some of the most powerful books, films, and plays in history. They aren't just entertaining, they are emotionally gripping. *Les Misérables* isn't just about revolution — it's about sacrifice, redemption, and hope. *The Road* isn't just a post-apocalyptic journey — it's about love and survival between a father and son. The best stories don't just tell us what happens — they make us feel it.

If you want to craft a story that touches readers on a deep level, you need to do more than just tell them how a character feels, you need to make them feel it for themselves. Here's how to infuse real emotion into your writing:

1. Create Relatable Characters Who Evoke Empathy.

The best way to make readers feel something is by introducing them to characters they can understand, relate to, or sympathize with. When characters are layered, complex, and display raw human emotions, readers are more likely to connect with them. Maybe your character is struggling with loss, fighting for a dream, or battling inner demons. When readers see their own experiences mirrored in a character, it pulls them in emotionally. The more your readers care about your characters' well-being, the more they'll feel every victory, loss, and heartbreak. Creating empathy allows readers to invest emotionally in the journey your characters are on.

How to make readers care about your characters:

- **Give them a deep, personal struggle** — whether it's internal (self-doubt, grief, guilt) or external (a failing relationship, an impossible goal, a devastating loss).

Example: In A Little Life by Hanya Yanagihara, Jude's traumatic past and self-destructive tendencies make readers feel his pain on a visceral level.

- **Let them feel joy as well as sorrow** — a story with only sadness won't resonate as deeply as one with moments of warmth and hope.

Example: In Anne of Green Gables, Anne's boundless optimism and imagination make her struggles feel even more poignant when she faces heartbreak.

- **Make their emotions feel earned** — if a character suddenly cries without buildup, readers won't feel the impact. Let their emotions develop naturally through the story's events.

How to apply this in your writing:

1. Ask: What does my character desire most? What's holding them back?
2. Give them moments of vulnerability, where they express fear, regret, or longing.

3. Let readers see what's at stake for them emotionally, not just physically.

2. Use Vivid Descriptions that Trigger Emotional Responses.

One of the most powerful tools you have as a writer is the ability to evoke emotion through vivid, sensory descriptions. Instead of simply telling your readers what's happening, show them in a way that stirs their emotions. Whether you're describing a scene of grief, joy, or tension, using sensory details - like the scent of a forgotten memory or the sharp sting of an unexpected betrayal - can make your writing come alive. The goal is to paint a picture that makes your readers feel the emotions along with your characters. A scene that appeals to the senses - what your character sees, hears, feels, and even smells - can trigger a visceral response that pulls readers deeper into the moment.

How to evoke emotion through description:

- **Use sensory language** — sight, sound, touch, taste, and smell can instantly evoke an emotional memory for a reader.

Example: Instead of writing, "She was heartbroken," show her sitting at the kitchen table, tracing the rim of her coffee cup with a shaking hand, staring at the untouched chair across from her.

- **Lean into metaphors and similes** — a strong comparison can make an emotion feel more tangible.

Example: "Grief settled on her shoulders like an old, familiar coat—one she never wanted to wear again."

- **Use setting to reinforce emotions** — the environment should reflect or contrast a character's mood.

Example: A character standing in a crowded, bustling city may feel lonelier than ever, emphasizing their isolation despite being surrounded by people.

Examples of emotionally rich writing:

- **Toni Morrison's Beloved:** Her lyrical descriptions of trauma and memory make the reader feel the weight of generational pain.

- **Kazuo Ishiguro's Never Let Me Go: Subtle,** restrained prose makes the slow, heartbreaking realization of the characters' fate all the more devastating.

- **Gabriel García Márquez's One Hundred Years of Solitude:** The dreamlike descriptions of love, longing, and loss add depth to the novel's magical realism.

How to apply this in your writing:

1. Instead of writing what a character feels, describe how it manifests physically.
2. Add sensory details that immerse the reader in the moment.
3. Use metaphors that enhance the weight and depth of the emotions.

3. Build Emotional Stakes that Keep Readers Invested.

Nothing keeps readers on the edge of their seats like emotional stakes. You need to make what's at risk matter to your characters, and, by extension, to your readers. This could be something tangible, like a character's life, or something more abstract, like love, identity, or hope. The higher the emotional stakes, the more tension and drama you create in the story. If readers believe that something important is on the line for your character, they'll be more emotionally invested in the outcome. They'll feel every twist, turn, and heartbreak right along with your character, making the stakes not only plot-driven but emotionally driven as well. If done right, these elements create a powerful bond between the story and the reader, one that stays with them long after they've turned the last page.

How to raise emotional stakes:

- **Make it personal** — stakes aren't just about saving the world; they're about saving something deeply meaningful to the character.

Example: In The Kite Runner by Khaled Hosseini, Amir's journey is fueled not just by external conflict but by his overwhelming guilt and need for redemption.

- **Ensure the stakes have irreversible consequences** — make your readers fear that what's at risk can't simply be undone.

Example: In Of Mice and Men by John Steinbeck, the devastating climax is powerful because the consequences are final.

- **Keep the stakes emotional, not just physical** — the most intense stakes are often internal struggles rather than just life-or-death scenarios.

Example: In Atonement by Ian McEwan, the emotional stakes revolve around guilt, regret, and the inability to undo the past.

Examples of high emotional stakes:

- **Edith Wharton's Ethan Frome:** The entire novel builds toward an emotional and tragic inevitability, with a sense of hopelessness growing in every scene.

- **Cormac McCarthy's The Road:** The father and son's desperate journey for survival is made more powerful by the emotional stakes of their love for each other.

- **Harper Lee's To Kill a Mockingbird:** The trial of Tom Robinson isn't just about justice — it's about morality, innocence, and the loss of childhood idealism.

How to apply this in your writing:

1. Ask: What's at stake for my character emotionally, not just physically?
2. Make sure the stakes escalate as the story progresses, what they risk should feel even greater.
3. Let readers fear for the character's outcome, uncertainty heightens emotional engagement.

TIP 24. WRITING FROM REAL LIFE: HOW TO TURN YOUR EXPERIENCES INTO STORIES

Your life experiences are a powerful tool for your writing because they can infuse your stories with authenticity, emotion, and depth. Whether you're writing fiction or memoir, your personal memories and feelings can serve as a foundation for compelling narratives. Here's how you can turn your real-life experiences into captivating stories:

1. Draw from Personal Emotions and Memories.

The emotions you've felt throughout your life are the heart of your stories. Whether it's love, loss, joy, or regret, tapping into your own emotional experiences can help create characters and situations that resonate deeply with readers. Think about a specific moment that made you feel something intense - maybe a time when you faced a tough decision or experienced a life-changing event. By reflecting on these emotions, you can craft scenes that feel raw and real, pulling readers into the experience. Your personal memories can serve as a wellspring for building emotional depth and complexity in your characters.

2. Use Real Locations or Events to Ground Your Story.

Sometimes, the setting of your story can be inspired directly by real-life places. Maybe it's the cozy coffee shop you visit every morning, the park where you've had meaningful conversations, or the bustling city where you once lived. These places can add richness to your writing and give your readers a sense of familiarity and immersion. By using real-world locations and events as a backdrop, you make the setting feel lived-in and authentic. You might not need to replicate the real-world scenario exactly, but drawing from those places can create a grounding sense of place in your story.

3. Make Sure to Fictionalize Details to Keep Things Fresh.

While it's tempting to recount your experiences verbatim, remember that good storytelling often requires creative license. Fictionalizing details allows you to shape the story, explore different "what if" scenarios, and make it more universally relatable. You don't have to reveal every personal detail or follow the exact events; instead, use them as a springboard for imagination. By altering names, locations, or key events, you can still tap into the essence of your experience without being tied down to the facts. This helps maintain both authenticity and artistic freedom, allowing you to create a narrative that is both personal and unique.

TIP 25. HOW TO CRAFT THE PERFECT ENDING

The ending of your story is one of the most powerful moments you'll write. This is because it's what lingers in a reader's mind long after they've turned the last page. A great ending leaves an impact, whether it's haunting, uplifting, shocking, or bittersweet. Readers remember endings because they define the final emotional experience of the journey you've taken them on.

Think of the most unforgettable endings in literature and film:

- The haunting ambiguity of George Orwell's 1984, where Winston succumbs to Big Brother's control, leaving readers unsettled and questioning the nature of power and resistance.

- The heartfelt closure in The Lord of the Rings, where Frodo sails away into the Undying Lands, symbolizing the cost of heroism and the bittersweet nature of moving on.

- The gut-punch revelation in Shutter Island, where Teddy Daniels realizes the truth of his identity, yet chooses to live in denial, leaving the audience to wonder whether he accepts his fate or escapes into madness.

A perfect ending doesn't necessarily mean a happy one. It means one that feels right, earned, and emotionally satisfying. But how do you achieve this?

Here are three essential techniques to nail your story's final moments.

1. Tie Up Loose Ends.

One of the most important aspects of a satisfying ending is making sure all the plot points and character arcs are resolved. Loose ends can leave readers feeling unsettled or frustrated, especially if they've invested time in the story. Whether it's resolving a central mystery, reuniting characters, or fulfilling promises made earlier in the story, these resolutions give the story a sense of completeness. But remember, this doesn't mean everything needs a neatly wrapped answer — some stories thrive on ambiguity — but major questions should be resolved in a way that feels earned.

Examples of satisfying resolutions:

- In Harry Potter and the Deathly Hallows, the series-long conflict with Voldemort concludes in an intense battle, and the epilogue offers a glimpse into Harry's future, providing closure while leaving room for imagination.

- In Pride and Prejudice, Elizabeth and Darcy's love story resolves in a way that satisfies the tension and character growth built throughout the novel.

- In The Road by Cormac McCarthy, the father's death is heartbreaking but inevitable, yet the boy's survival and the hope of human connection offer closure.

How to apply this:

1. Identify the main conflicts and character arcs — make sure they come to a natural resolution.
2. Don't introduce new conflicts in the last moments — instead, bring clarity to the ones you've already built.
3. If some questions are left unanswered, ensure that what remains ambiguous still feels purposeful and intentional.

2. Provide Closure but Leave Room for Imagination.

While it's important to wrap up the main plot, a great ending also leaves readers with something to think about. Providing closure for the characters and their journey is essential, but you don't need to spell out every detail. Leave a few questions unanswered or allow for some ambiguity to engage readers' imaginations. A thoughtful ending might suggest what could happen next without explicitly stating it, allowing readers to imagine the future for themselves. This technique works especially well in literary fiction, mystery, thrillers, and dystopian novels, where ambiguity enhances the impact of the story.

Examples of endings that leave room for imagination:

- In The Great Gatsby, Nick reflects on Gatsby's life and the American Dream, leaving readers contemplating the novel's themes rather than offering a definitive resolution.

- In Life of Pi, the ending challenges the reader to decide which version of the story is true, forcing them to question perception, belief, and reality.

- In Inception, the final shot of the spinning top leaves audiences debating whether Cobb is still dreaming or has returned to reality.

How to apply this:

1. End with a lingering thought, question, or possibility.
2. Hint at what's next for the characters, rather than stating it outright.
3. Trust your readers and let them interpret certain aspects for themselves.

3. Make Sure It's Emotionally Satisfying.

The emotional impact of your ending can define how readers remember your story. Whether it's a bittersweet farewell, a hard-won victory, or a moment of personal growth, your ending should evoke an emotional response. Ensure that it feels true to the characters and the journey they've been on. An emotionally satisfying ending can leave readers feeling fulfilled, connected to the characters, and moved by the story.

The emotional weight of an ending depends on the story's themes and the stakes you've built. If a novel has been leading toward a tragic, inevitable downfall, forcing a forced happy ending will feel false. If a story has been about hope, transformation, and overcoming struggles, a bleak ending may feel unsatisfying.

Examples of emotionally impactful endings:

- In To Kill a Mockingbird, Scout walks Boo Radley home, reflecting on understanding others through their perspective, bringing an emotionally rich, full-circle moment to the novel.

- In Of Mice and Men, George's devastating choice to kill Lennie is heartbreaking but inevitable, cementing the novel's themes of sacrifice and mercy.

- In The Book Thief, the final moments reveal the heartbreaking but hopeful outcome of Liesel's life, emphasizing the power of words and resilience.

How to apply this:

1. Ask yourself: *What is the final emotional note I want my readers to feel?*
2. Stay true to the characters and themes and don't force an unnatural resolution.
3. End in a way that feels earned, whether it's hopeful, tragic, or open-ended.

Just remember, a great ending doesn't just close the book, it makes readers feel something. Whether it's resolution, reflection, or wonder, your final moments should carry emotional weight and stay true to the journey you've built.

PART 6: ADVANCED WRITING SKILLS

This section covers more sophisticated storytelling techniques, including subtext, foreshadowing, and the use of symbolism. Writers will also learn how to craft suspense, write powerful emotional scenes, and master pacing to keep readers engaged.

TIP 26. HOW TO WRITE CONFLICT THAT MOVES THE PLOT FORWARD

Conflict is the driving force behind every great story. It challenges characters, heightens tension, and keeps readers emotionally invested in what happens next. Without conflict, stories fall flat, leaving no reason for readers to turn the page.

Think of some of the most memorable books and films, they all thrive on compelling conflict:

- In The Kite Runner, Amir's internal guilt over betraying his childhood friend fuels his emotional arc and ultimately shapes the entire story.

- In The Dark Knight, Batman and the Joker's ideological battle isn't just about good vs. evil, it's a deep moral conflict that forces Batman to question his own limits.

- In The Hunger Games, Katniss isn't just fighting for survival, she's fighting against an oppressive system that forces children to kill for entertainment, making her struggle far greater than just her own life.

Conflict isn't just about fighting, arguing, or obstacles, it's about change, consequences, and character growth. The most effective conflicts push the story forward rather than merely filling space. Here's how to ensure your story's conflict is meaningful, impactful, and moves the plot in a compelling direction.

1. Create Obstacles that Challenge Your Characters.

Your protagonist should never have an easy path to success. Introduce roadblocks that force them to adapt, make difficult choices, or rethink their beliefs. If your protagonist achieves their goals too easily, there's no sense of struggle, and without struggle, there's no reason for readers to care. The best conflicts introduce roadblocks that force characters to adapt, make difficult choices, or question their own beliefs.

There are two main types of obstacles:

- **External conflict** – Physical barriers that prevent a character from achieving their goal.

- **Internal conflict** – Psychological struggles that create emotional turmoil and personal growth.

Examples of effective obstacles:

- **External Conflict:** In The Lord of the Rings, Frodo's journey isn't just long, it's filled with literal and emotional roadblocks. He faces enemies, betrayal, exhaustion, and the psychological weight of carrying the One Ring.

- **Internal Conflict:** In Atonement by Ian McEwan, Briony's guilt and inability to undo her childhood mistake create lasting, painful consequences, shaping the entire novel.

- **Combined Conflict:** In Breaking Bad, Walter White faces external enemies (cartels, police) while struggling with internal moral dilemmas (his descent into ruthlessness and ego).

How to apply this:

1. Ask: What's stopping my character from getting what they want?
2. Introduce increasingly difficult choices. Force them to pick between two equally risky options.
3. Don't make things easy. Growth comes from struggle.

2. Make the Stakes High so the Conflict Matters.

Conflict doesn't work unless there's something to lose. If failure has no real impact, tension disappears, and the reader has no reason to be invested. The best conflicts make characters risk something important, whether that's their life, their reputation, their love, or their sense of self.

Stakes can be:

- **Life-threatening:** A character faces physical danger or survival challenges (The Road by Cormac McCarthy).

- **Emotionally devastating:** A character risks losing a loved one, their dream, or their identity (La La Land, Me Before You).

- **Morally conflicting:** A character must make an impossible choice (Game of Thrones, Ned Stark choosing between honor and survival).

Examples of high stakes:

- In The Handmaid's Tale, Offred's life is at constant risk. One wrong move, and she could be executed or worse. The stakes are deeply personal and politically charged.

- In Of Mice and Men, George's choice to protect Lennie is gut-wrenching because the stakes are both tragic and inevitable.

- In The Fault in Our Stars, Hazel and Augustus don't just risk love, they risk heartbreak in the face of terminal illness.

How to apply this:

1. Ask: What's the worst possible consequence if my character fails?
2. Raise the stakes as the story progresses. Each challenge should make the risk bigger and more personal.
3. If the stakes aren't high enough, make the consequences of failure more severe.

3. Ensure the Conflict Pushes the Plot Forward, not Sideways.

Every conflict should change something in the story. Every argument, setback, or challenge should push the protagonist toward a new choice, revelation, or direction. If a conflict happens but nothing in the story changes, it's just filler.

Think about:

- Does this conflict reveal something new about my characters?

- Does it make them rethink their approach?

- Does it force them to make a decision that moves them closer (or further) from their goal?

Examples of conflict that moves the plot forward:

- In Harry Potter and the Goblet of Fire, the Triwizard Tournament challenges Harry in ways that push him toward uncovering Voldemort's return. It's not just about survival; it's about uncovering deeper secrets.

- In Gone Girl, every conflict between Nick and Amy reveals more about their toxic marriage and manipulative personalities, keeping the reader guessing.

- In To Kill a Mockingbird, the courtroom conflict doesn't just provide drama, it fundamentally changes Scout's understanding of race, justice, and morality.

How to apply this:

1. Ensure that every conflict has consequences. It should lead to character growth, a new discovery, or a change in direction.
2. Remove conflicts that don't add value. If a fight, challenge, or obstacle doesn't lead to a revelation or action, cut it.
3. Make sure each conflict builds upon the last, creating rising tension rather than repetition.

Keep in mind, without struggle, there's no story. The most compelling conflicts do more than create drama — they drive the narrative, challenge characters to grow, and keep readers invested. When executed well, conflict doesn't just add excitement, it leaves a lasting impact.

TIP 27. THE ART OF SUBTEXT IN WRITING: WHAT'S LEFT UNSAID

Subtext is the invisible thread that runs beneath the surface of a story, adding depth, complexity, and emotional weight. It's the difference between a scene that tells the audience exactly what's happening and one that allows them to feel the tension, interpret the emotions, and uncover hidden meanings on their own.

Some of the most critically acclaimed films and TV shows master the art of subtext, using silence, body language, and indirect dialogue to reveal far more than words ever could. Think of the unspoken grief in *Manchester by the Sea*, the heavy pauses in *Breaking Bad*, or the loaded, coded conversations in *The Godfather*. These moments stay with us not because of what is said, but because of what isn't.

So, how can you infuse your writing with subtext that enhances your storytelling? Here are three powerful techniques.

1. Hint at Emotions Without Saying Them Outright.

One of the biggest mistakes writers make is over-explaining emotions. Instead of telling your readers exactly what a character is feeling, let them experience it through the character's actions, body language, or even what they choose not to say. If a character is sad, it's tempting to write "She felt heartbroken." But the most powerful writing allows the audience to feel that heartbreak rather than stating it outright.

Example from TV & Film:

- In Mad Men, Don Draper often suppresses his emotions, but his pain is evident in the way he pours his drink, the way he adjusts his tie before walking into a room, or how his voice slightly breaks when talking about his past. His emotions are never directly stated, yet the audience feels them deeply.

- In Manchester by the Sea, Casey Affleck's character, Lee Chandler, is a man broken by his past. Instead of monologues explaining his grief, his reluctance to talk, his avoidance of eye contact, and his stiff body language all hint at his overwhelming sorrow.

How to apply this in your writing:

1. Use body language to hint at internal struggles ("She poured another drink, but her hand trembled slightly.").
2. Have characters avoid certain topics. Sometimes, what they refuse to discuss says more than what they actually say.
3. Show emotional tension through small, deliberate actions (He clenched his jaw. She adjusted her sleeves, avoiding his gaze.)

2. Use Dialogue that Suggests More than it Reveals.

Some of the best dialogue isn't about what's being said, it's about what's being avoided, hinted at, or spoken in half-truths. The best screenwriters use this to their advantage, making conversations layered with hidden meaning and tension. A seemingly casual conversation can carry weight and layers when there's tension beneath the words. Imagine two characters talking about the weather, but there's a pause every time the conversation shifts to something more personal. The silences, the way certain words are stressed, and the rhythm of the conversation all create a tension that communicates unspoken truths. Dialogue doesn't have to be straightforward; it can be a dance of suggestion.

Example from TV & Film:

- In Breaking Bad, Walter White and his wife, Skyler, often engage in seemingly mundane conversations about dinner or work, but beneath the surface, it's a battle of control and deception. Skyler knows Walter is lying, and her short, clipped responses carry more weight than direct accusations ever could.

- In The Godfather, when Michael Corleone tells his brother Fredo, "You're nothing to me now," there's a subtle undercurrent of betrayal and heartbreak. He doesn't need to scream or explain because his detached delivery says everything.

How to apply this in your writing:

1. Avoid direct exposition. Let characters talk around an issue instead of confronting it head-on.
2. Use pauses, interruptions, and subtext-laden remarks to build tension ("I heard you had a late night," he said, stirring his coffee. "Must've been important.").
3. Let emotions slip through in the way words are said, not just the words themselves (She forced a smile. "I'm fine.").

3. Let The Reader's Imagination Fill in the Gaps.

Great storytelling respects the reader's intelligence. Instead of spoon-feeding every detail, leave room for the reader to interpret, to make connections, and to imagine what's happening beneath the surface. Instead of over-explaining or giving every detail, leave enough room for the reader to create their own mental image of the scene or the character's emotions. This active participation creates a deeper engagement with the story and lets readers feel like they're discovering hidden layers on their own.

Example from TV & Film:

- In No Country for Old Men, the fate of a major character is never explicitly shown. In fact, the scene cuts away before the moment of impact. This lack of closure leaves viewers uneasy, forcing them to grapple with what happened. The unknown is far more unsettling than a direct explanation.

- In Lost in Translation, the final whispered exchange between Bill Murray and Scarlett Johansson is left unheard. Instead of telling the audience what was said, the mystery makes the moment even more profound because it becomes personal to each viewer.

How to apply this in your writing:

1. Instead of stating everything outright, let implications, half-revealed truths, and unanswered questions deepen the scene.
2. Leave room for interpretation. Don't explain every action (She picked up the phone, stared at the screen, then set it down without dialling. What does this mean? Let the reader decide.).

3. Trust the power of suggestion. The right hint can be more powerful than a full explanation.

In conclusion, subtext transforms good writing into something immersive, thought-provoking, and emotionally rich. When used effectively, it allows readers to engage more deeply with your characters and story, making them active participants rather than passive consumers.

TIP 28. HOW TO WRITE A COMPELLING VILLAIN

A great villain isn't just a roadblock for the hero, they are the driving force of conflict, the emotional anchor of tension, and sometimes, the most unforgettable character in a story. The best villains challenge the protagonist's beliefs, push them to their limits, and force them to grow.

Some of the most iconic villains in TV and film are remembered not because they are evil, but because they are complex, layered, and deeply human. Think of:

- **The Joker** (The Dark Knight) – An agent of chaos whose philosophy forces Batman to question his own moral code.

- **Anton Chigurh** (No Country for Old Men) – A relentless hitman whose eerie calm and twisted logic make him terrifying.

- **Cersei Lannister** (Game of Thrones) – A ruthless queen whose every action is rooted in protecting her family, making her both monstrous and tragically relatable.

- **Killmonger** (Black Panther) – A villain with a painful past and an understandable motivation, making his ideology compelling even if his methods are brutal.

So, how do you craft a villain that is more than just an obstacle? By giving them purpose, complexity, and depth.

1. Give Them a Clear Motivation, Make Them Believable.

Your villain's actions need to be driven by something deeper than just a desire to "do evil." Maybe they want power, revenge, or to protect someone they love, but whatever it is, it should make sense in the context of who they are and what they've experienced. They need to believe that they are justified in their actions, even if their methods are extreme. By establishing a strong motivation, you make the villain more than just a force of chaos. They become a character with a purpose, someone whose actions are rooted in their own beliefs, past, and desires. This makes them feel like a real, complex person, not just a caricature of evil.

Examples of Villains with Strong Motivations:

- Thanos (Avengers: Infinity War) – His goal isn't to destroy for the sake of destruction. He truly believes he is saving the universe by wiping out half of its population. His motivation is rooted in logic and his own experiences, making his perspective chillingly rational.

- Gus Fring (Breaking Bad) – A businessman and crime lord who operates with precision, not out of senseless cruelty, but because power and control are what keep him alive. His need for revenge against Hector Salamanca is deeply personal, giving depth to his calculated demeanour.

- Magneto (X-Men) – He isn't just "evil"; his motivations stem from his trauma as a Holocaust survivor. His belief that humans will always try to exterminate mutants makes his actions extreme, but understandable.

How to apply this in your writing:

1. Ask: What does my villain want, and why do they believe it is right?
2. Give them a backstory that explains their perspective, but don't over-explain, leave room for intrigue.
3. Make their goal conflict directly with the protagonist's, creating a meaningful struggle.

2. Show Their Complexity. No One is Purely Evil.

Real people aren't all good or all bad, and neither should your villains be. The most compelling antagonists are the ones who feel real — they have vulnerabilities, moments of doubt, and even moments of kindness. The best villains make readers question whether they are truly evil or simply the product of their circumstances. Show the struggles they've faced, their insecurities, and perhaps the moral code they follow. A villain who believes they are the hero of their own story is far more compelling than one who's simply wicked for the sake of being wicked.

Examples of Complex Villains:

- **Walter White (*Breaking Bad*)** – He starts as a desperate man trying to provide for his family, but his descent into villainy is slow and tragic. We see his love for his family, his moments of guilt, but also his growing pride and greed.

- **The Governor (*The Walking Dead*)** – A seemingly charismatic leader who believes he is protecting his people, but his paranoia and brutality turn him into a tyrant. His arc makes us question: Is he a monster, or a man doing what he believes is necessary?

- **Hans Landa (*Inglourious Basterds*)** – A Nazi officer who is disturbingly charming, polite, and even humorous — making his ruthlessness even more terrifying. His complexity comes from his intelligence and his ability to manipulate, making him unpredictable.

How to apply this in your writing:

1. Give your villain moments of vulnerability: a lost love, a personal trauma, or a moral dilemma.
2. Show them making choices that are understandable, even if they are wrong.
3. Let them have redeeming qualities, maybe they are fiercely loyal to someone, have a strong sense of justice (even if warped), or display genuine emotion.

3. Let Their Actions Challenge the Hero in a Meaningful Way.

A villain isn't just an obstacle for the hero to overcome; they should push the protagonist to grow, change, and even question their beliefs. Their actions should create moral dilemmas, force the hero to make tough choices, or test their limits. The best villains make the hero stronger, smarter, or more determined as they learn from their encounters with them. Whether it's an ideological clash or a personal vendetta, the villain's actions must create stakes that are meaningful for the hero's journey.

They should reflect the hero's fears, flaws, or worst-case scenario. When a villain represents what the protagonist could become, the conflict becomes personal rather than just external.

Examples of Villains as Mirrors:

- **Darth Vader (*Star Wars*)** – Once a Jedi, he represents what Luke Skywalker could become if he gives in to his anger and fear.

- **Ra's al Ghul (*Batman Begins*)** – He and Bruce Wayne both want to rid Gotham of corruption, but Ra's is willing to destroy the city to save it, while Bruce refuses to cross that moral line.

- **Javier Bardem's Silva (*Skyfall*)** – He is a fallen agent, representing what James Bond could become if he allowed himself to be consumed by betrayal and revenge.

How to apply this in your writing:

1. Ask: How does my villain challenge my protagonist's values?
2. Make them force the hero to change, whether through temptation, direct confrontation, or ideological opposition.

3. Consider making the villain someone the protagonist admires, respects, or even loves, creating emotional stakes.

4. Make Them Unpredictable and Memorable.

The scariest, most compelling villains are unpredictable. If readers always know what your villain will do next, the tension disappears. Great villains keep both the protagonist and the audience on edge—they should be capable of shocking decisions, cunning strategies, or moments of chilling calmness.

Examples of Unpredictable Villains:

- **The Joker (*The Dark Knight*)** – His lack of a clear motive makes him terrifying—he thrives on chaos, and his erratic behavior keeps both Batman and the audience constantly uneasy.

- **Anton Chigurh (*No Country for Old Men*)** – His coin-flipping method of deciding life or death makes his character unsettling — he sees fate as random, making his actions feel both arbitrary and inevitable.

- **Hans Gruber (*Die Hard*)** – At first, he seems like just another terrorist, but his sophisticated, calculated approach and his ability to stay one step ahead make him iconic.

How to apply this in your writing:

1. Give your villain a unique, chilling trait, an unusual habit, a specific belief, or a ritual that makes them distinct.

2. Make them one step ahead. They should challenge the protagonist in ways that feel impossible to overcome.
3. Keep them strategic and intelligent. A smart villain is always scarier than a reckless one.

In the end, a story is only as strong as its conflict, and the best conflicts come from great villains. A well-crafted antagonist is more than just an obstacle, they are a force that shapes the hero's journey, tests their morals, and keeps the tension high.

TIP 29. WHY WRITERS NEED TO READ (AND WHAT TO READ)

Great writers know that reading is just as important as writing! Whether you're a seasoned novelist or just starting out, reading deeply and widely can transform your writing. Here's why it's essential for writers to read:

1. It Improves Your Vocabulary and Writing Style.

The more you read, the more words and phrases you encounter, which helps build your vocabulary. But it's not just about having more words at your disposal, it's about seeing how other writers use language to create impact. Reading a variety of genres and styles exposes you to different ways of expressing emotions, building suspense, and creating rich imagery. You'll absorb these techniques naturally, and they'll start to influence your own writing voice. Reading challenges you to expand your linguistic toolkit and helps you find your own unique way to communicate on the page.

2. It Shows You How Other Writers Structure Their Work.

Every writer has their own approach to structure, pacing, and narrative. By reading different books - whether it's a novel, short story, or article - you'll start to recognize the building blocks of storytelling. Notice how tension builds over time, how subplots weave into the main narrative, and how characters evolve. By deconstructing the work of others, you'll gain insights into how to construct your own stories, experiment with different narrative techniques, and understand the flow of a well-written piece. It's like having a personal blueprint for building your own writing projects.

3. It Sparks Creativity and New Ideas.

Reading opens your mind to new worlds, perspectives, and ideas. It exposes you to different cultures, historical periods, and emotional journeys, which can all inspire your own work. A well-crafted plot twist, a unique character arc, or an unusual writing style can prompt you to think differently about your own stories. It can push you to take creative risks and come up with fresh ideas that you may not have considered before. Reading also helps you recognize patterns in storytelling and identify what resonates with you, which can give you a deeper sense of direction for your own writing.

TIP 30. HOW TO WRITE A STRONG OPENING SCENE

The opening scene of your story is more than just the first page, it's your best chance to hook the reader, introduce your world, and set the tone for everything that follows. A great beginning should immediately draw readers in, spark curiosity, and establish a reason to keep turning the pages. Think of some of the most iconic opening scenes in film and literature:

- The eerie, unsettling prologue of Jaws, where a swimmer is dragged underwater, setting up the horror and tension of the story without revealing too much.

- The tension-filled first scene of Inglourious Basterds, where a Nazi officer interrogates a farmer hiding Jewish refugees beneath his floorboards. The quiet conversation is polite on the surface but layered with suspense, making the inevitable reveal all the more terrifying.

- The high-stakes energy of The Dark Knight, which opens with a meticulously executed bank heist, introducing the Joker's cunning and unpredictability before we even see his face.

Your first few pages (or even your first few lines) should make the reader want to know what happens next. But how do you do that? Here are three essential techniques to crafting a strong, unforgettable opening scene.

1. Start with Action or Intrigue.

Your opening scene doesn't need to start with explosions, battles, or chases, but it shouldn't be slow or meandering either. You want to throw the reader into something compelling, whether it's an unsettling event, an emotional confrontation, or a small mystery that demands answers.

A strong opening raises questions in the reader's mind. They don't need all the answers right away, but they should feel intrigued enough to keep reading.

Examples of openings that hook immediately:

- "It was a bright cold day in April, and the clocks were striking thirteen." – 1984 by George Orwell (This strange, slightly wrong detail instantly unsettles the reader.)

- "The man in black fled across the desert, and the gunslinger followed." – The Gunslinger by Stephen King (This one line promises an intense pursuit and makes us wonder: Who is the man in black? Why is he being chased?)

- The opening of Breaking Bad drops us right into the action: Walter White, half-dressed and panicked, driving an RV through the desert with sirens blaring behind him. We have no context, but we need to know what led to this moment.

How to apply this in your writing:

1. Open in the middle of something happening, an argument, a discovery, a difficult choice.
2. Start with a sentence or detail that feels slightly off, slightly wrong, or intriguing enough to make readers curious.
3. Avoid excessive exposition, don't explain everything at once. Let the reader discover information naturally.

2. Establish Your Setting and Characters Quickly.

Your opening scene should immerse readers in your world, whether that's a futuristic city, a medieval kingdom, or a small suburban town. Readers don't need pages of world-building, but they do need enough detail to understand where they are and who they're following.

One of the best ways to introduce setting and character at the same time is through action, movement, and sensory details. Instead of simply describing the world, show your character interacting with it.

Examples of immersive openings:

- **Nocturnal Animals (Austin Wright)** – The novel begins with a woman receiving a mysterious manuscript from her ex-husband. The setting is ordinary, but the presence of this unexpected letter creates tension.

- **Blade Runner 2049** – The film begins establishing the bleak, dystopian setting through visuals — endless wastelands, a silent tension in the air — as K, the protagonist, arrives at a lonely farmhouse. The mood and environment tell us about the world before a word is spoken.

- **American Psycho (Bret Easton Ellis)** – Patrick Bateman describes a billboard featuring a missing person's poster as he walks through New York, giving readers a glimpse into the dark, detached world he inhabits.

How to apply this in your writing:

1. Show your character interacting with their world. Are they sneaking through a crowded marketplace? Rushing

through a rainstorm, or standing in an eerily silent room?
2. Use sensory details (sound, smell, temperature, atmosphere) to make the setting come alive.
3. Let the world reveal itself naturally. Instead of long exposition, show the reader what they need to know through character movement and dialogue. Keep descriptions lean and relevant, focus on what matters in the moment.

3. Create a Hook that Makes Readers Want More.

Your opening should not only introduce the scene but also promise something exciting to come. A strong hook could be a mysterious question, a compelling conflict, or an unexpected event that demands answers. This is the moment when the reader's curiosity is piqued, and they're hooked into the narrative. Whether it's a shocking revelation, a sudden twist, or a character on the brink of an important decision, your opening should make them crave more of the story.

A strong hook can be:

- **A mysterious question** (Why is this character running? What just happened? What will they do next?)

- **A compelling conflict** (Two characters are arguing, and we don't yet know why.)

- **An unexpected event** (Something shocking or unusual happens right away.)

Examples of strong opening hooks:

- In Fight Club, the book opens with the narrator holding a gun in his mouth, while Tyler Durden explains how everything will soon be destroyed. Immediately, we wonder: How did he get here? Who is Tyler Durden? What is about to happen?

- In The Girl with the Dragon Tattoo, we start with an old man receiving an anonymous package — inside is a pressed flower. The repetition of this strange event for 40 years raises immediate intrigue.

- In No Country for Old Men, the opening describes the eerie, matter-of-fact killing of a police officer by Anton Chigurh, setting the stage for the unsettling violence that follows.

How to apply this in your writing:

1. End the first page (or paragraph) with an unanswered question — something that forces the reader to keep going.
2. Introduce conflict or stakes immediately — even if they are small at first.
3. Avoid long, drawn-out introductions — instead, tease the reader with something they need to know more about.

In conclusion, your opening scene isn't just a starting point, it's the initial invitation into your story. It should pull readers in, intrigue them, and make them desperate to know more. And when done well, a strong opening doesn't just introduce a story, it makes the reader unable to walk away from it.

PART 7: STRUCTURE AND STYLE

This chapter explores essential storytelling techniques, from using flashbacks without confusing readers and crafting realistic dialogue to overcoming writer's block. You'll also learn the importance of editing and revising and how to create a strong, compelling protagonist to ensure your story is both engaging and polished.

TIP 31. HOW TO USE FLASHBACKS WITHOUT CONFUSING YOUR READER

Flashbacks are a powerful storytelling tool, allowing writers to reveal key moments from the past that shape the present. When used effectively, they can deepen character development, enhance emotional impact, and provide crucial context. However, if poorly executed, they can confuse readers, disrupt pacing, and weaken the momentum of your story.

Some of the most compelling books and films master the art of flashbacks, seamlessly integrating them into the narrative. Consider:

- **The Godfather Part II** – The film interweaves Michael Corleone's present-day struggles with his father Vito's rise to power, showing how past choices echo into the present.

- **Big Little Lies** (Liane Moriarty) – The novel's structure revolves around flashbacks that slowly reveal the truth behind a murder, keeping the reader intrigued.

- **Lost** (TV Series) – The show uses flashbacks (and later flash-forwards) to provide key character backstories, allowing us to understand their present-day actions and conflicts.

The key to writing effective flashbacks is ensuring they feel necessary, seamless, and easy to follow. Here's how to use them without losing your reader.

1. Make Sure They Serve the Plot.

Flashbacks should never be inserted just for the sake of showing the past; they should be essential to the current narrative. Whether it's revealing a character's backstory, explaining a crucial event, or uncovering a secret that ties into the present conflict, the flashback should add something essential to the current plot.

Ask yourself:

- Does this flashback change how the reader views the present events?
- Does it reveal something that moves the story forward?
- Would the story feel incomplete or weaker without it?

Examples of flashbacks that serve the plot:

- **Atonement** (Ian McEwan) – A crucial misunderstanding in the past shapes the entire novel, and flashbacks gradually reveal the consequences of one fateful decision.

- **The Book Thief** (Markus Zusak) – Flashbacks highlight Liesel's past traumas, making her present fears and relationships more powerful.

- **The Haunting of Hill House** (Netflix series) – The show brilliantly weaves between past and present, showing how childhood trauma affects the adult lives of its characters.

How to apply this in your writing:

1. Don't dump unnecessary backstory. Only include flashbacks that add emotional depth, tension, or insight into present conflicts.
2. Avoid stopping the momentum of your story for long-winded flashbacks, instead, make sure they connect with the present moment.
3. If the flashback doesn't reveal anything new or necessary, consider cutting it or incorporating the information more subtly.

2. Clearly Signal When You're Switching to a Flashback.

One of the biggest mistakes writers make with flashbacks is transitioning into them too abruptly, making it hard for readers to follow the shift in time. If the transition isn't clear, the reader can easily get confused, and the flow of the story will be disrupted. You can use specific cues, like a change in tense, time markers (e.g., "years ago," "in the past"), or visual/formatting changes like italics or chapter breaks to indicate the shift. These subtle signals will help the reader mentally prepare for a change in time and allow them to distinguish between the present narrative and past events.

Techniques for signalling a flashback:

- **Change in verb tense** – If your main story is in past tense, you can shift the flashback to past perfect (*had been, had gone*) to clarify the time jump.

- **Time markers** – Use phrases like *"Years ago…,"* *"That summer…,"* or *"Before everything changed…"* to orient the reader.

- **Scene breaks or formatting changes** – Italics, section breaks, or an entirely new chapter can visually separate flashbacks.

- **A sensory trigger** – A character sees an old photograph, hears a familiar song, or revisits a place that sparks a memory.

Examples of seamless flashback transitions:

- **In The Night Circus** (Erin Morgenstern), flashbacks are marked by dates and locations, helping the reader track multiple timelines.

- **In The Lovely Bones** (Alice Sebold), the protagonist, who narrates from the afterlife, smoothly dips in and out of memories using sensory triggers.

- **In The Handmaid's Tale** (Margaret Atwood), Offred's memories of her past life are triggered by small moments in her present, making the shifts feel organic.

How to apply this in your writing:

1. Make sure the first sentence of the flashback clearly establishes the time shift (*"It had been ten years since she last saw him."*).
2. Use formatting or line breaks to visually separate flashbacks from present-day narration.
3. Don't make the reader guess. Always provide context clues to indicate they've entered a memory.

3. Keep Them Short and Relevant.

Flashbacks work best when they're concise. A lengthy flashback can slow down the pacing of your story and disengage readers.

Focus on the key moments that are directly relevant to the current storyline. Instead of offering a whole backstory, zero in on specific scenes that reveal important character motivations or plot details. Flashbacks should provide just enough information to move the story forward, and once they've done that, return to the present narrative to keep the pace steady.

A good rule of thumb is:

- Keep flashbacks concise and impactful.
- Focus on key moments that matter to the story.
- Return to the present as soon as you've delivered the necessary information.

Examples of well-executed flashbacks:

- **Gone Girl** (Gillian Flynn) – Alternates between diary entries from the past and present-day events, slowly revealing hidden truths.

- **It** (Stephen King) – Uses brief but haunting flashbacks to show childhood fears that still haunt the characters as adults.

- **Slaughterhouse-Five** (Kurt Vonnegut) – The protagonist experiences flashbacks involuntarily, mirroring his trauma, but the novel keeps them short and tied to the main narrative.

How to apply this in your writing:

1. Instead of telling an entire backstory, pick one or two defining moments to illustrate a character's past.
2. If a flashback drags on too long, consider breaking it up into smaller fragments throughout the story.

3. Once the flashback has served its purpose, return to the present before losing momentum.

TIP 32. HOW TO WRITE REALISTIC DIALOGUE

Dialogue is one of the most powerful tools in storytelling — it brings characters to life, reveals personality, builds relationships, and drives the plot forward. When done well, dialogue feels natural and immersive, making readers feel like they're listening in on a real conversation. But when dialogue sounds stiff, forced, or overly polished, it can break immersion and weaken character development.

Think about some of the most memorable conversations in books, films, and TV. They don't just transfer information, they create tension, evoke emotions, and deepen character relationships:

- The casual yet layered conversations in *Pulp Fiction* – Tarantino's dialogue feels real, not just because of how the characters speak, but because their seemingly mundane discussions (like the "Royale with Cheese" scene) make them feel like real people.

- The quick, overlapping dialogue in *Gilmore Girls* – The fast-paced, witty exchanges define the characters' personalities and relationships, making their banter feel alive.

- The haunting silences in *No Country for Old Men* – The moments of what's not said in tense conversations (like

Anton Chigurh's coin toss scene) create more suspense than any direct statement ever could.

So, how do you write dialogue that sounds real, reveals character, and enhances your story?

1. Make It Sound Natural. Remember People Don't Speak in Perfect Sentences!

Real-life conversations are messy. People interrupt each other, speak in fragments, and sometimes trail off mid-sentence. In writing, avoid making your dialogue too polished or formal. Let characters use slang, mumble, or have moments of uncertainty. It's also important to incorporate pauses or stumbles in speech, like "uh" or "you know," to mirror how people naturally communicate. This kind of casual, imperfect speech helps the reader feel like they're eavesdropping on a real conversation rather than reading a script or story.

Examples of Natural vs. Stiff Dialogue:

Unnatural, overly polished dialogue:

"I am very upset with you right now, Jacob. I cannot believe you lied to me. That was a serious mistake, and now I do not know if I can trust you anymore."

More natural, realistic dialogue:

"Are you serious, Jacob? You lied to me? I mean... how am I supposed to trust you now?"

Ways to make dialogue sound more natural:

- Use contractions (*"I am going to the store"* → *"I'm going to the store"*).

- Let characters interrupt each other in fast-paced or heated conversations.

- Use pauses, hesitations, and filler words where appropriate (*"Uh... I don't know about that."* or *"You know, I never really thought about it that way."*).

- Keep it concise. People rarely speak in long, uninterrupted paragraphs.

How to apply this in your writing:

1. Read your dialogue out loud, if it sounds robotic or unnatural, rewrite it.
2. Imagine two actors performing the scene, would their conversation flow smoothly or sound forced?
3. Listen to real conversations, observe how people talk and incorporate those speech patterns into your writing.

2. Show Character Emotion Through Tone and Word Choice.

What a character says is just as important as *how* they say it. The tone they use, whether it's sharp, sarcastic, soft, or upbeat, can convey a wide range of emotions without explicitly stating them. For example, if a character is frustrated, they might say, "Sure, whatever," but the tone could be cold or clipped. On the other hand, if they're excited, their words might be rushed, and they might exclaim things like, "I can't believe this is happening!" Use your character's specific way of speaking to reflect their emotional state and personality.

Examples of Emotion in Dialogue:

1. Frustration

- *"Oh, great. Just what I needed."* (sarcastic, clipped tone)
- *"You're seriously telling me this now?"* (angry, accusatory)
- *"Forget it. I don't even care anymore."* (resigned, bitter)

2. Excitement

- *"I can't believe this is happening!"* (fast-paced, exclamation)
- *"Oh my God, tell me everything!"* (enthusiastic, eager)
- *"This is unreal. Are we actually doing this?"* (incredulous, breathless)

3. Sadness/Disappointment

- *"Yeah. No, it's fine. I get it."* (defeated, avoiding confrontation)
- *"I thought… I don't know. Never mind."* (hesitant, holding back)
- *"I guess I should've seen this coming."* (resigned, hurt)

How to apply this in your writing:

1. Instead of writing *"She was upset,"* show it through word choice, sentence structure, and punctuation.
2. Let emotion slip through tone, not just explicit statements (*"I'm fine" can mean 100 different things depending on how it's said*).

3. Avoid over-explaining emotions and trust your reader to pick up on subtext.

3. Let the Dialogue Reveal Something About the Character or Situation.

Dialogue isn't just about getting information across; it's a tool for deeper storytelling. What a character says - or doesn't say - can reveal a lot about them. Are they evasive or blunt? Do they use humor to mask their vulnerability? Are they trying to hide something? Dialogue can also highlight the dynamics of a scene. Is there tension between characters? Is one character more dominant in the conversation? Let your dialogue show more than just the surface conversation, and use it to expose character traits, conflicts, or hidden agendas.

Examples of Dialogue That Reveals Character & Conflict:

1. A character who is avoiding confrontation:

- *"Oh… yeah, I totally forgot about that."* (They didn't forget, but they don't want to admit it.)
- *"Look, can we talk about this later?"* (They're uncomfortable and stalling.)

2. A character with a sharp, sarcastic personality:

- *"Oh, sure. Because that went so well last time."*
- *"I'd love to help, but unfortunately, I'm allergic to stupidity."*

3. Two characters with underlying tension:

- *Person A:* "You okay?"

- *Person B:* "Why wouldn't I be?" (Defensive, something is obviously wrong.)
- *Person A:* "You're not still mad, are you?"
- *Person B:* "Did I say I was mad?" (Passive-aggressive, avoiding direct confrontation.)

How to apply this in your writing:

1. Instead of telling readers about a character's personality, show it through their speech patterns, tone, and choice of words.
2. Use subtext. Not everything has to be directly stated. What characters don't say can be just as important as what they do.
3. Let tension the build. Interruptions, miscommunications, and unspoken words can create intrigue and drama.

TIP 33. HOW TO OVERCOME WRITER'S BLOCK

Writer's block can be frustrating, but it's just a temporary hurdle, not the end of your creative journey! Here's how to push through and get back into the flow of writing:

1. Take a Break and Let Your Brain Reset.

Sometimes, the best way to break through writer's block is to step away from your work for a bit. Your brain needs time to process, rest, and recharge. This isn't about procrastination; it's about giving yourself permission to not think about writing for a moment. Go for a walk, read a book, listen to music, or just relax. Often, when you return to your writing after a break, you'll find that your mind is clearer, and fresh ideas will come to you more easily. A brief mental reset can be the key to unlocking new inspiration.

2. Change Your Writing Environment for Fresh Inspiration.

A change of scenery can do wonders for your creativity. If you've been writing in the same place for a while, try moving to a different spot, whether it's a cozy café, a park bench, or a new room in your house. The shift in your surroundings can spark new ideas and offer a fresh perspective. Being in nature or a different setting can also help clear mental fog and stimulate your senses. Sometimes, a new environment can help shake up your routine and reignite your passion for writing.

3. Try Freewriting or a Prompt to get the Words Flowing.

If you're feeling stuck, don't wait for the perfect idea to strike. Instead, try freewriting, set a timer for 10 minutes and just write whatever comes to mind, no matter how random. The goal is to break through the block and get words on the page. If freewriting doesn't appeal, use a writing prompt. Prompts can provide a spark for new ideas and help you start writing without the pressure of perfection. You might be surprised where a random prompt can take you!

TIP 34. THE IMPORTANCE OF EDITING AND REVISING

Great writing isn't about getting it perfect on the first try. It's all about editing and revising to make your work shine! Here's why editing is crucial to your writing process:

1. You'll Catch Errors and Improve Clarity.

The first draft is often a rough outline of your ideas, and it's normal for mistakes to slip through. Editing is where you catch the small errors that may distract or confuse readers, whether it's typos, grammar mistakes, or awkward sentence structures. But it's not just about fixing those errors. Editing gives you the opportunity to refine the clarity of your writing. Are your ideas clearly expressed? Is your message coming across the way you intend? Taking the time to revise ensures that everything flows smoothly and that your readers can easily follow along.

2. It Gives You the Chance to Refine Your Voice.

Your writing voice is unique, and editing allows you to fine-tune it. Whether your voice is humorous, poetic, or straightforward, editing helps you make it more consistent and authentic. During revisions, you can assess whether your character's dialogue feels true to who they are or if your narrative tone aligns with the atmosphere you want to create. Editing helps strip away any unnecessary fluff and lets your true voice shine through, making your writing more impactful and memorable.

3. Editing Helps Improve Pacing and Flow.

Pacing is vital to keeping readers engaged, and editing is where you adjust the rhythm of your story. Are there parts that drag on too long? Are there scenes that feel rushed or disjointed? During the revision process, you can smooth out awkward transitions, tighten scenes, and make sure the action flows at just the right speed. Editing allows you to find the balance between description, dialogue, and action so that your story moves along in a way that keeps readers hooked.

TIP 35. HOW TO WRITE A STRONG PROTAGONIST

Your protagonist is the anchor of your story, the character readers will invest in, relate to, and follow from beginning to end. A well-crafted protagonist drives the plot, carries the emotional weight of the narrative, and keeps the reader engaged. Without a compelling main character, even the most intricate plots can fall flat.

The most memorable protagonists, whether in books, TV, or film, aren't just strong because of their abilities, but because of their desires, flaws, and personal transformations. Consider:

- **Elizabeth Bennet** (*Pride and Prejudice*) – She is smart, independent, and strong-willed, but her pride and quick judgments create obstacles in her romantic journey.

- **Walter White** (*Breaking Bad*) – A mild-mannered chemistry teacher turned drug kingpin, whose tragic flaw (his ego and hunger for power) leads to his downfall.

- **Katniss Everdeen** (*The Hunger Games*) – She doesn't seek to be a hero but is forced into leadership and rebellion, struggling with trauma, survival, and protecting those she loves.

- **Sherlock Holmes** (*Arthur Conan Doyle's series*) – Brilliant and methodical but also arrogant and socially distant, making him both fascinating and flawed.

A great protagonist isn't just someone who goes on a journey. They are someone whose internal struggles, external conflicts, and ultimate transformation make that journey unforgettable.

1. Give Them a Clear Goal They're Striving For.

A strong protagonist has a clear, motivating goal that drives their actions throughout the story. This goal doesn't have to be grandiose, but it should be something important to them, whether it's personal growth, saving someone they love, or achieving a dream. A clear goal helps ground the reader in the character's motivations and gives the story a sense of direction.

Goals can be:

- **External** – Winning a competition, escaping a dangerous situation, solving a mystery.

- **Internal** – Seeking self-acceptance, overcoming fear, learning to trust.

- **A Combination** – A character might be searching for a missing loved one (external goal) while also struggling with guilt over past mistakes (internal conflict).

Examples of protagonists with clear goals:

- Frodo Baggins (*The Lord of the Rings*) – His goal is to destroy the One Ring, but his personal struggle with its corrupting power makes the journey far more intense.

- Jay Gatsby (*The Great Gatsby*) – His goal is to win back Daisy, but it's fuelled by his obsession with the past and illusion of the American Dream.

- Harry Potter (*Harry Potter series*) – His goal is to defeat Voldemort, but throughout the series, he also battles self-doubt, loneliness, and the burden of expectations.

How to apply this in your writing:

1. Ask: *What does my protagonist want more than anything?*
2. Ensure their goal is important, personal, and urgent, as it should drive their choices.
3. Create obstacles that force them to fight for their goal, making their journey engaging.

2. Show Their Flaws and Vulnerabilities.

Perfect characters are rarely relatable. A strong protagonist is one who is multi-dimensional, with both strengths and weaknesses. Showcasing their flaws, whether it's a fear, a bad habit, or a personal insecurity, makes them more human and relatable. Vulnerabilities give them depth and make them more complex. Readers will empathize with their struggles and feel more connected to their journey. A protagonist without flaws can seem unrealistic, and without vulnerability, there's little room for growth or transformation.

Some common types of protagonist flaws:

- **Emotional flaws** – Fear of intimacy, insecurity, arrogance.
- **Behavioral flaws** – Impulsiveness, stubbornness, dishonesty.
- **Moral dilemmas** – Doing the wrong thing for the right reason.

Examples of protagonists with compelling flaws:

- **Tony Stark** (*Iron Man*) – Brilliant but reckless and self-absorbed, forced to confront his ego and responsibility.

- **Eleanor Shellstrop** (*The Good Place*) – Selfish and morally bankrupt at first, but slowly learns to care for others.

- **Holden Caulfield** (*The Catcher in the Rye*) – Struggles with alienation, cynicism, and a fear of growing up, making him both frustrating and deeply human.

How to apply this in your writing:

1. Ask: *What personal flaw makes my protagonist's journey harder?*
2. Make sure their flaws create obstacles, something they need to overcome to succeed, something they will learn and grow from.
3. Let them fail and struggle. A perfect and flawless protagonist makes for an unrealistic and boring protagonist.

3. Make Sure They Grow Throughout the Story.

One of the most satisfying aspects of storytelling is watching a character evolve. A strong protagonist should not be the same person at the end of the story as they were at the beginning. This transformation can be dramatic or subtle, but it should be earned. A great character arc involves internal change, shaped by the obstacles and choices they face throughout the story. Whether the growth is positive (self-discovery, redemption, empowerment) or negative (moral corruption, loss of innocence, downfall), the key is that the protagonist is transformed by their experiences.

Examples of strong character arcs:

- **Neville Longbottom** (*Harry Potter series*) – Starts as a timid, clumsy boy who lacks confidence, but through perseverance and courage, he grows into a brave leader who stands up to Voldemort when it matters most. His arc is subtle but powerful, showing that heroism doesn't always come from natural talent but from inner strength and resilience.

- **Elizabeth Swann** (*Pirates of the Caribbean series*) – Begins as a governor's daughter, bound by societal expectations, but over the course of the films, she transforms into a fierce, independent pirate leader who defies expectations and fights for her own destiny.

- **Mulan** (*Disney's Mulan*) – Starts as an insecure young woman who doubts her abilities, but through her journey, she proves herself as a warrior, earns the respect of an entire army, and redefines what it means to bring honor to her family.

- **Shrek** (*Shrek series*) – Begins as a self-isolated ogre who believes he doesn't need anyone, but through his relationship with Donkey and Fiona, he learns to let down his walls, accept love, and embrace companionship.

- **Joe March** (*Little Women*) – Starts as an ambitious writer who is fiercely independent and resistant to change, but by the end of the novel, she comes to understand the complexities of love, family, and sacrifice, growing in ways that don't compromise her values but enhance them.

How to apply this in your writing:

1. Ask: *What lesson does my protagonist need to learn?*
2. Make sure their growth happens through struggles and choices, not suddenly at the end.
3. Ensure their arc feels organic. A characters growth should be gradual, not instant.

A compelling protagonist evolves as the story unfolds, making their journey not just believable, but emotionally satisfying for the reader.

PART 8: KEEPING READERS ENGAGED

This chapter delves into essential techniques for keeping readers engaged, including crafting unforgettable plot twists, building suspense, staying creatively inspired, developing compelling romantic relationships, and creating a gripping opening hook that draws readers in from the very first line.

TIP 36. HOW TO WRITE A PLOT TWIST

A well-executed plot twist is one of the most powerful tools in storytelling. It can shock readers, change everything they thought they knew about the story, and make them eager to reread earlier chapters just to spot the clues they missed. The best twists don't just surprise, they feel inevitable in hindsight, leaving readers with that satisfying *"How did I not see that coming?"* moment.

Think of some of the most iconic plot twists in literature and film:

- **The Sixth Sense** (*1999*) – The shocking revelation that Dr. Malcolm Crowe was dead all along, a twist that was brilliantly foreshadowed through subtle details that only make sense upon rewatching.

- **Gone Girl** (Gillian Flynn) – Just when the reader thinks they understand Amy's disappearance, the novel flips everything upside down by revealing Amy is alive and has orchestrated the entire thing.

- **Fight Club** (Chuck Palahniuk) – The narrator and Tyler Durden are revealed to be the same person, a twist that completely recontextualizes the entire book.

- **Harry Potter and the Prisoner of Azkaban** (J. K. Rowling) – The shocking moment when Sirius Black is revealed to be Harry's godfather and not the villain he was believed to be.

The key to a great plot twist is that it feels both unexpected and completely logical at the same time. Here's how to craft a twist that will leave your readers stunned yet satisfied.

1. Plant Subtle Clues Earlier in the Story.

A great plot twist isn't just a random surprise; it's a moment that feels earned. To make it truly shocking yet satisfying, you need to plant subtle clues throughout the story. These clues can be small, almost imperceptible details, like a character's odd behavior, a mysterious object, or a seemingly insignificant line of dialogue. The key is to lay the groundwork early so that when the twist is revealed, the reader can look back and see how it makes sense, even if they didn't see it coming. These subtle hints keep the twist from feeling forced and allow your readers to experience that "aha!" moment.

Techniques for foreshadowing a twist effectively:

- **Seemingly insignificant details** – A minor character's offhand remark, an object mentioned in passing, or an unusual habit can later take on greater meaning. (*Example: In The Sixth Sense, Bruce Willis's character never interacts with anyone except the boy—an unnoticed clue that he's actually dead.*)

- **Misdirection** – Make readers focus on one thing while subtly hinting at something else. (*Example: In Gone Girl, the focus is on Nick's suspicious behavior, diverting attention from the fact that Amy is orchestrating everything.*)

- **Character inconsistencies** – Have a character act slightly off in a way that isn't immediately suspicious but makes sense once the twist is revealed. (*Example: In Fight Club,* *the narrator frequently blacks out or forgets events, hinting that Tyler Durden is his split personality.*)

- **Symbolism and imagery** – Repeating an image or phrase that takes on a new meaning after the twist is revealed.

How to apply this in your writing:

1. Identify key details that can later take on new meaning.
2. Use misdirection. Lead readers to expect one outcome while subtly setting up another.
3. Test your twist by rereading earlier sections. Does it reward close readers without making the reveal too obvious?

2. Make Sure the Twist is Believable, not Forced.

A plot twist should never feel like it's being pulled out of thin air. While it should surprise your readers, it should also feel logical in the context of the story. The twist should emerge naturally from the events, character actions, and themes you've developed throughout the narrative. It shouldn't contradict anything that has come before or seem like it exists just for shock value. If a twist is too outlandish or comes out of nowhere, it can break the immersion and leave your readers feeling unsatisfied. A great plot twist emerges naturally from the story, meaning it aligns with the world, the characters, and the themes you've already built.

How to make a twist feel believable:

- It must be rooted in the story's logic. If your twist contradicts established facts, readers will feel cheated instead of impressed. (Example: In The Usual Suspects, the revelation that Verbal Kint is Keyser Söze works because the film subtly builds up the mystery around Söze's identity without contradicting earlier information.)

- It must align with character actions. If a twist completely contradicts a character's personality, it will feel forced. (Example: If a heroic character suddenly betrays their friends for no reason, readers will feel manipulated unless their motivations were subtly hinted at earlier.)

- It should make earlier scenes more meaningful. A great twist doesn't erase the story—it enhances it. (Example: In The Prestige, the twist that Borden had a twin all along makes every scene of his erratic behavior suddenly make sense.)

How to apply this in your writing:

1. Ask: *Does this twist fit the story's established world and characters?*
2. Make sure the twist doesn't feel random. It should arise naturally from the narrative.
3. Re-read your story and see if the twist enhances earlier scenes instead of contradicting them.

3. Ensure It Has a Lasting Impact on the Characters and Plot.

The twist should do more than just surprise the reader, it should significantly affect the characters and the direction of the story. After the twist is revealed, the characters should react in ways that feel true to their nature, and the plot should shift in response. The twist can change a character's motivations, relationships, or even the tone of the story. Ideally, the twist should make readers rethink everything they thought they knew about the plot or characters. It's not just about the shock factor; it's about how the twist reshapes the world you've built and makes everything that follows more engaging.

Examples of twists that reshape the story:

- **Severus Snape's true loyalty** (Harry Potter and the Deathly Hallows) – The revelation that Snape was protecting Harry all along reshapes our understanding of his character and deepens the emotional impact of his arc.

- **The murder twist in Psycho** – When Marion Crane is unexpectedly killed early in the movie, it forces the entire story to shift, making Norman Bates the central figure.

- **The identity twist in The Others** – The shocking reveal that Grace and her children are the actual ghosts doesn't just surprise, it changes the way we interpret every event leading up to it.

How to apply this in your writing:

1. Ask: Does this twist change the stakes or character relationships?
2. Ensure the characters' responses to the twist feel realistic. How do they react to this major revelation?
3. Let the twist create new tension or challenges. It should push the story forward, not just serve as a one-time shock.

In the end, a great plot twist isn't just about surprise, it's about execution. When done well, it deepens the story, recontextualizes earlier events, and keeps readers thinking about your book long after they've finished it.

TIP 37. HOW TO WRITE SUSPENSE AND KEEP READERS ON THE EDGE OF THEIR SEAT

Suspense is the invisible thread that pulls readers deeper into your story, keeping them eager to turn the page, desperate to know what happens next. Whether you're writing a thriller, mystery, horror, or even a drama, suspense creates tension, raises stakes, and forces readers to anticipate what's coming.

Some of the greatest stories master suspense by making readers feel like something crucial is just out of reach — an unanswered question, a secret waiting to be revealed, a decision hanging in the air. Consider:

- **Gone Girl** (Gillian Flynn) – The story keeps readers on edge by slowly unravelling the truth behind Amy Dunne's disappearance, playing with deception, unreliable narration, and unexpected twists.

- **Silence of the Lambs** (Thomas Harris) – The tension between Clarice Starling and Hannibal Lecter is psychological suspense at its finest, as Lecter knows more than he reveals, making every conversation a battle of wits.

- **A Quiet Place** (film) – Suspense is created not just through monsters, but through silence, vulnerability, and the constant risk of exposure.

But suspense isn't just about big action moments. It's about what's left unsaid, what's lurking beneath the surface, and the sense that danger is just around the corner. Here's how to master suspense and make your readers feel the tension in every scene.

1. Build Tension Gradually Through Character Conflict.

Suspense isn't just about action, it's about emotional stakes and unresolved conflict. To create tension, slowly ramp up the conflicts between your characters. Let their relationships unravel or become strained as the story progresses. This could be a character's internal struggle, a misunderstanding, or even a growing rivalry. By layering small moments of conflict, you draw readers into the emotional stakes and make them wonder what will happen when things inevitably come to a head. Remember, if the readers aren't emotionally invested in the characters, they won't care about the stakes. That's why suspense works best when it's deeply personal, rooted in internal struggles, interpersonal tension, and unresolved conflict.

Ways to create suspense through character conflict:

- **Internal tension** – A protagonist may be torn between two impossible choices (saving a loved one vs. exposing the truth), creating suspense through their inner turmoil.

- **Rising friction between characters** – Two characters with opposing goals or hidden agendas create underlying tension in every interaction. (Think of Walter White and Jesse Pinkman's strained partnership in Breaking Bad).

- **Secrets and deception** – When a character hides something from another (or even from the reader), every conversation becomes an opportunity for revelation or betrayal.

- **A ticking clock** – A looming deadline or countdown forces characters into difficult situations, increasing stress and urgency. (A detective with 24 hours to solve a case before the killer disappears).

Examples of character-driven suspense:

- In The Girl with the Dragon Tattoo, the tension builds as journalist Mikael Blomkvist gets closer to solving a decades-old crime, while Lisbeth Salander harbors her own dark past that threatens to surface.

- In Breaking Bad, Walter White's descent into criminality creates suspense because every decision inches him closer to exposure — the audience knows his lies will unravel, but when and how?

- In Rebecca (Daphne du Maurier), the suspense is rooted in the narrator's growing insecurity about her place in Manderley, as the shadow of her husband's deceased wife, Rebecca, looms over her marriage.

How to apply this in your writing:

1. Create internal conflict that forces the protagonist into tough decisions.
2. Introduce interpersonal tension — make conversations loaded with subtext and hidden meaning.
3. Let secrets linger — build suspense by delaying key revelations.

2. Leave Questions Unanswered and Make Readers Crave More.

Suspense thrives on mystery. You don't have to give your readers all the answers at once, try to keep them guessing! Withhold key information and drop subtle hints that suggest there's more to the story than meets the eye. Is there a secret the protagonist doesn't know yet? Why is a secondary character acting suspiciously? What's really going on behind the scenes? These unanswered questions create a sense of curiosity and tension that pushes readers to keep going. The more they wonder, the more invested they become in finding out the truth, driving them to read further.

Ways to keep readers guessing:

- **Withhold key information** – Reveal things in fragments, leaving gaps for readers to fill. (Why does the old man never talk about his past? Why did the victim receive a cryptic letter before disappearing?)

- **Use unreliable narrators** – Keep readers questioning whether they can trust what's being told. (Gone Girl plays with perspective shifts to make readers constantly reevaluate the truth).

- **Foreshadow without giving everything away** – Drop tiny details that hint at something larger, making the reader feel like they missed something important. ("She locked the drawer and slipped the key into her pocket. No one could ever see what was inside." - What's in the drawer? Readers will keep reading to find out.*)

- **Create false leads and red herrings** – Make readers think they've figured it out, only to realize they were wrong. (Agatha Christie's And Then There Were None expertly misleads readers, keeping them guessing who the killer is until the final reveal).

Examples of unanswered questions that build suspense:

- In Shutter Island, every clue Teddy Daniels finds leads to more questions rather than answers, making the reader feel trapped in the same psychological maze as the protagonist.

- In Inception, the final scene leaves viewers questioning whether Cobb is still in a dream, keeping the tension alive long after the credits roll.

- In Stranger Things, the mystery of Eleven's origins and the Upside Down unfolds piece by piece, drawing the audience deeper into the suspense.

How to apply this in your writing:

1. Reveal just enough to keep readers intrigued but hold back the full truth.
2. Drop subtle clues that readers won't recognize as important until later.
3. End chapters on unanswered questions, compelling readers to keep going.

3. Keep the Pacing Tight, with Moments of High Stakes.

The pacing of your story is crucial in building suspense. You need to maintain a sense of urgency and tension throughout the narrative. Quick, sharp scenes with unexpected twists can help keep the reader's heart racing. Just as important is knowing when to slow down, these moments of quiet reflection, when paired with high-stakes scenes, amplify the tension. You can alternate between breathless action and moments of suspense where the stakes feel personal and emotional. Every moment should have a sense of risk or danger, even if it's internal. Your pacing should reflect this, don't let the tension drop for too long, and keep the threat of consequences looming. If the pacing drags for too long, the tension dissipates. But if the action is non-stop, it can become exhausting. The key is to balance fast-paced, high-stakes moments with slower, tension-filled buildup.

Ways to maintain strong pacing:

- **Short, sharp sentences in high-stakes moments** – Creates a sense of immedacy. ("The door creaked. She held her breath. Footsteps. Closer now.")

- **Slow, drawn-out tension in key scenes** – When something crucial is about to happen, delay the reveal to make readers squirm. (A detective reaches for the doorknob, but before opening it, he notices something unusual...).

- **Use sensory details** – Let readers feel the moment—describe the pounding of a heartbeat, the creak of the floorboards, the cold sweat on the character's skin.

- **Alternate between action and reflection** – After a major event, let characters absorb what's happened. This brief slowdown makes the next suspenseful moment hit even harder.

Examples of strong pacing in suspense:

- In The Road (Cormac McCarthy), the tension comes from quiet, slow dread — the father and son are constantly under the threat of unseen dangers, and every interaction feels like it could turn deadly.

- In A Quiet Place, the suspense builds because of what the audience doesn't hear — every small sound becomes a possible death sentence, making even silent moments full of tension.

- In The Girl on the Train, the novel's fragmented, non-linear timeline keeps readers piecing things together, increasing suspense as they realize the protagonist may be unreliable.

How to apply this in your writing:

1. Use shorter sentences in intense moments to quicken the pace.
2. Slow down key moments to heighten the reader's anticipation.
3. Keep a sense of urgency—even in quiet moments, let the reader feel the tension.

TIP 38. HOW TO STAY INSPIRED AS A WRITER

Inspiration is the fuel of creativity, but like any resource, it can run low, especially when you're knee-deep in a project, facing self-doubt, or struggling with writer's block. The key to long-term creative success isn't waiting for inspiration to strike, it's learning how to cultivate it and keep the creative fire burning even when motivation wanes.

Great writers know that inspiration can come from anywhere. It can come from a book, a song, a conversation, or even a quiet moment of reflection. Consider:

- Stephen King has spoken about how everyday observations spark his ideas, such as how Misery was inspired by a nightmare during a flight.
- J. K. Rowling developed Harry Potter after a train delay forced her to sit and imagine a world of wizards.
- Quentin Tarantino constantly draws inspiration from classic films, reinterpreting old ideas in bold, fresh ways.

Creativity isn't about waiting for the perfect idea. It's about actively seeking and nurturing it. Here's how to stay inspired, no matter what stage of writing you're in.

1. Read Books, Watch Movies, And Consume Art.

Creativity doesn't exist in a vacuum, the more you absorb, the more ideas you have to work with. Reading books, watching movies, listening to music, or even observing the world around you helps fuel inspiration by exposing you to new ideas, perspectives, and emotions.

Ways to draw inspiration from other creative works:

- **Read widely and across genres** – A mystery novel might spark an idea for a sci-fi story, or a historical drama might inspire a fantasy setting. (*Example: George R. R. Martin drew inspiration from the real-life War of the

Roses to shape the power struggles in Game of Thrones.)

- **Watch movies and TV shows with a writer's eye** — Pay attention to storytelling techniques, pacing, dialogue, and character arcs. (Example: Christopher Nolan's Inception explores layered storytelling, inspiring writers to play with nonlinear narratives.)

- **Engage with art and music** — A painting, a song, or even a dance performance can evoke emotions that trigger new story ideas. (Example: The song "Being for the Benefit of Mr. Kite!" by The Beatles was inspired by an old circus poster Paul McCartney found, proving that even small things can spark entire worlds.)

- **Observe real life** — Sometimes the best inspiration comes from the ordinary moments. These can be things like overhearing a conversation, watching someone on the subway, or reflecting on past experiences.

How to apply this in your writing:

1. Keep a "Spark Notebook" where you jot down quotes, observations, and ideas that stand out to you.
2. Try writing prompts inspired by books or films. What if a side character got their own story? What if a scene was rewritten from a different perspective?
3. Visit museums, listen to music, or explore new places. You never know what might ignite a new idea.

2. Surround Yourself with Creative People.

Writing can be a solitary endeavor, but inspiration often thrives in collaboration, conversation, and shared creativity.

Surrounding yourself with other writers, artists, and storytellers keeps your imagination active and motivates you to keep creating.

Ways to find creative energy from others:

- **Join a writing group** – Whether in-person or online, connecting with other writers helps keep ideas flowing, provides accountability, and gives you fresh perspectives. (Example: The Inklings was a writers' group including C.S. Lewis and J.R.R. Tolkien, where they discussed and refined their works.)

- **Engage in creative discussions** – Talking about books, films, or creative struggles can spark new insights and push you past writer's block.

- **Collaborate on projects** – Even if you're a novelist, try collaborating with a filmmaker, a musician, or an artist, as it can introduce new ways of thinking and storytelling.

- **Attend workshops, readings, or conferences** – Being in a space dedicated to creativity can reignite passion and expose you to fresh ideas. (Example: Screenwriters often find inspiration by attending film festivals and hearing directors discuss their process.)

How to apply this in your writing:

1. Find an accountability partner, someone who checks in on your progress and keeps you motivated.
2. Have "idea jam sessions" with creative friends where you throw out random story concepts. This can lead to unexpected breakthroughs.

3. Surround yourself with people who challenge and inspire you. Creativity is energy that feeds off itself. The more creativity you surround yourself with, the easier you will find it.

3. Write Every Day, Even when You're not Feeling Inspired.

The biggest myth about inspiration is that it only comes when you feel like writing. In reality, writing consistently, even when uninspired, keeps the creativity alive and prevents you from getting stuck in a rut.

Why writing everyday matters:

- **It turns writing into a habit** – The more you write, the easier it becomes to slip into a creative mindset. (Example: Haruki Murakami treats writing like a daily workout—showing up consistently strengthens the creative muscle.)

- **It helps break through writer's block** – Sometimes the act of writing sparks new ideas, even if you don't start with inspiration. (Example: Stephen King writes every day, believing that creativity flows best when it's treated like a job, not a waiting game.)

- **It prevents perfectionism from taking over** – If you only write when you're feeling "ready," you may never finish a project. Daily writing removes the pressure of always needing to be inspired.

Ways to keep writing, even when uninspired:

- **Freewriting** – Set a timer for 10 minutes and write whatever comes to mind—no pressure, no editing.

- **Use writing prompts** – A random idea can turn into something unexpected. (Example: Margaret Atwood's The Handmaid's Tale began as a small idea she jotted down in a notebook.)

- **Change up your routine** – If you're stuck, try writing in a different location, changing your writing time, or experimenting with a new format (e.g., poetry, journaling, dialogue-only scenes).

- **Lower your expectations** – Not every writing session has to produce something great. The goal is to keep the creative gears turning.

How to apply this in your writing:

1. Set a small daily goal, even 100 words a day keeps momentum going.
2. Keep an "Inspiration File", store unfinished ideas, stray thoughts, or half-written scenes to revisit later.
3. Trust that inspiration often comes in the process of writing, not before it.

TIP 39. HOW TO WRITE ROMANTIC RELATIONSHIPS IN YOUR STORY

Romantic relationships bring depth, emotional complexity, and stakes to a story, but they need to feel authentic, earned, and meaningful to truly resonate with readers. A forced or unrealistic romance can make characters feel one-dimensional, while a well-developed one can enhance character arcs, drive the plot, and add emotional weight to the narrative.

Think about some of the most iconic literary and cinematic romances, they're not just about two people falling in love; they're about growth, tension, challenges, and choices:

- **Elizabeth Bennet and Mr. Darcy** (Pride and Prejudice) – Their romance is built on misunderstandings, pride, and personal growth, making the eventual love story feel deeply satisfying.

- **Katniss Everdeen and Peeta Mellark** (The Hunger Games) – Their relationship is not just about romance but survival, manipulation, and emotional dependence, making it layered and compelling.

- **Jim and Pam** (The Office) – Their slow-burn romance is rooted in small moments, genuine friendship, and personal challenges, making their eventual union feel earned rather than forced.

- **Jack and Rose** (Titanic) – Their love story raises the emotional stakes of the plot, turning Jack's sacrifice into one of the most gut-wrenching moments in cinema.

Romantic relationships in fiction work best when they feel natural, contribute to character development, and serve the story. Here's how to write a romance that feels real, emotional, and compelling.

1. Develop the Relationship Slowly. No Insta-Love!

One of the biggest mistakes writers make is rushing into romance too quickly. Insta-love — where two characters meet and instantly fall head-over-heels — often feels shallow, unrealistic, and unearned.

Real relationships take time to build. Love develops through trust, shared experiences, emotional vulnerability, and overcoming challenges together. A romance that slowly evolves over the course of the story feels more authentic and emotionally rewarding.

Ways to build a slow-burn romance:

- **Start with attraction, but don't rush emotional intimacy** – Attraction is different from love. Let the characters be intrigued by each other, but don't have them declare love after one conversation.

- **Use small, meaningful moments** – Romantic tension thrives in the little things: brushing hands, stolen glances, teasing banter, moments of protectiveness. (*Example: Jim putting a teapot full of inside jokes in Pam's Christmas gift in The Office.)

- **Let conflict play a role** – A strong romance is forged through struggles, misunderstandings, and personal challenges. (Example: Elizabeth and Darcy's initial conflict makes their eventual love feel more rewarding.)

- **Show growth before commitment** – Love is about learning and growing. Maybe one character has trust issues, and the other helps them open up. Maybe one is reckless, and the other teaches them caution. Their journey together should be a process, not an instant spark.

How to apply this in your writing:

1. Instead of writing "They fell in love," SHOW why they fall for each other.
2. Use small, intimate moments to build their bond over time.
3. Give them obstacles to overcome together, reinforcing their emotional connection.

2. Show the Characters' Individual Growth.

The best romantic relationships in stories feature characters who evolve both individually and as a couple. Each character should have their own arc, personal challenges, dreams, or insecurities that they work through. As they grow and change, the relationship should mirror that growth. Perhaps one character learns to open up emotionally, or another becomes more confident in their decisions. The romance shouldn't just be about two people coming together; it should also reflect their individual journeys and how their relationship helps them become better versions of themselves.

Examples of characters growing within a romance:

- **Hazel and Augustus** (The Fault in Our Stars) — Both characters are battling illness and mortality, but their romance isn't just about love — it's about finding meaning, embracing life, and learning to live despite fear. Augustus pushes Hazel to see the world beyond her illness, while Hazel teaches Augustus to understand the realities of life and death in a way he hadn't before.

- **Allie and Noah** (The Notebook) – Their love story spans decades, but their relationship isn't just about passion — it's about identity, choices, and self-discovery. Allie struggles with societal expectations and what she truly wants, while Noah learns the meaning of persistence, devotion, and sacrifice. Their relationship forces them both to grow, with Noah becoming more emotionally open and Allie learning to make decisions based on her own desires, rather than what others expect.

- **Harry and Sally** (When Harry Met Sally) – This romance is rooted in personal growth and self-awareness. Both characters go through years of failed relationships, heartbreak, and self-discovery before they finally realize they are meant for each other. Sally's independence and emotional depth challenge Harry's cynicism about love, while Harry helps Sally understand that love doesn't always come in the way we expect. Their relationship feels authentic because it develops naturally as they mature, change, and overcome their personal baggage.

How to apply this in your writing:

1. Ask: Who is this character outside of the romance?
2. Make sure each character has personal goals and struggles. They should exist as full people, not just "the love interest."
3. Show how the relationship challenges them to grow, rather than just being an easy love story.

3. Make Sure the Romance Adds to the Overall Plot.

Romantic subplots should never feel like they're just there for the sake of romance. The relationship should be integral to the main story, driving character motivations and influencing key events. The romance can create emotional stakes, introduce conflicts, or even challenge a character's goals or beliefs. Whether it creates internal conflict, brings characters closer to their goals, or forces them to make tough choices, the romance should move the plot forward, making it an essential element rather than an optional add-on.

Ways romance can add to the main plot:

- **It creates emotional conflict** – A character's feelings might complicate their goals. (Example: In Romeo and Juliet, their love directly contradicts their families' rivalry, creating the central conflict.)

- **It raises the stakes** – If a character falls in love, they now have someone they want to protect, fight for, or risk things for. (*Example: Jack sacrificing himself for Rose in Titanic.)

- **It changes a character's perspective** – Maybe falling in love makes a character question their beliefs or values. (Example: In La La Land, Mia and Sebastian's romance is about choosing between love and career, making their ending more bittersweet.)

- **It plays into the theme of the story** – If your story is about redemption, self-discovery, or loss, the romance should reflect those themes.

Examples of romance serving the main plot:

- In A Star is Born, the romance isn't just love, it's about fame, addiction, and self-destruction, adding depth to the tragedy.

- In Casablanca, Rick and Ilsa's love story isn't just about romance, it's about sacrifice, wartime morality, and choosing duty over desire.

- In Spider-Man 2, Peter Parker struggles between being a hero and having a normal life with Mary Jane, making the romance an integral part of his character arc.

How to apply this in your writing:

1. Ask: Does this romance impact the plot, or could I remove it without consequence?
2. Make sure the relationship creates challenges, choices, or stakes for the characters.
3. Let the romance add emotional weight to the story rather than just existing as filler.

TIP 40. HOW TO WRITE AN EFFECTIVE OPENING HOOK

Your opening hook is your first and best chance to grab your reader's attention. It sets the tone, establishes intrigue, and most importantly, compels readers to keep turning the pages. A weak opening risks losing your audience before they even get past the first paragraph, while a strong one immerses them instantly into your world.

Think about some of the most iconic openings in literature and film — they don't waste time. They pull you in immediately, making you ask questions, feel tension, or experience something powerful:

- **"Call me Ishmael."** (Moby-Dick) – A simple yet intriguing introduction that hints at a larger story without revealing too much.

- **"It was a bright cold day in April, and the clocks were striking thirteen."** (1984) – The strange, unsettling detail of "thirteen" immediately signals that something is off in this world.

- **"I believe in America."** (The Godfather) – A bold statement that immediately suggests themes of power, loyalty, and the American Dream.

A great opening hook isn't just about beautiful writing, it's about making the reader ask questions, feel tension, and crave more information. Here's how to craft an irresistible opening that ensures readers can't put your story down.

1. Start with a Question that Piques Curiosity.

A great hook often begins with a question that makes the reader want to know more. It could be an intriguing thought, a mystery, or a dilemma that demands an answer. One of the best ways to hook your audience is by immediately planting a question in their mind. If they're intrigued, they'll keep reading because they need to know the answer. This could be a literal question, an unusual statement, or a situation that demands explanation.

Techniques to spark curiosity:

- **Introduce an unusual scenario** – ("What if you woke up one morning with no memory of your life?")

- **Make a bold, unexplained statement** – ("The first time I died, I was 27 years old.")

- **Open with a contradiction** – ("She hated him more than anything, which made it inconvenient that she was in love with him.")

Examples of openings that create immediate curiosity:

- *"Last night I dreamt I went to Manderley again."* (Rebecca, Daphne du Maurier) – This line immediately makes readers ask: What is Manderley? Why is it only in a dream now?

- *"All happy families are alike; each unhappy family is unhappy in its own way."* (Anna Karenina, Leo Tolstoy) – This statement implies deep family drama ahead.

- *"We were somewhere around Barstow on the edge of the desert when the drugs began to take hold."* (Fear and Loathing in Las Vegas, Hunter S. Thompson) – The surreal setting and unpredictable narration make readers want to know what happens next.

How to apply this in your writing:

1. Open with a situation that needs an answer. Make the reader curious and slightly off-balance.
2. Introduce an unexplained event, thought, or character that immediately makes the reader ask why.
3. Keep it short but powerful. Your first line should feel like a key turning in a lock.

2. Introduce Conflict or Mystery Immediately.

Right from the start, you need to show that something is at stake. Whether it's a looming threat, a personal dilemma, or a mysterious event, introducing conflict or mystery early on makes the story feel urgent. Conflict could be an external threat, like a character running from danger, or an internal struggle, such as a decision that needs to be made. A sense of mystery can also work wonders, leave small clues or questions that hint at something bigger, ensuring readers feel invested in finding out more. A strong opening doesn't just introduce a character or setting, it introduces tension. Conflict is what drives all great stories, and starting with a moment of tension ensures immediate engagement.

Ways to introduce conflict early:

- **Drop the reader into an urgent situation** – ("I had exactly ten minutes to disappear before they found the body.")

- **Show a character at a breaking point** – ("She had rehearsed this moment a hundred times, but now that it was happening, her hands wouldn't stop shaking.")

- **Begin with an unsettling or mysterious event** – ("The note on the table simply read: 'I know what you did.'")

Examples of openings that introduce conflict immediately:

- *"Someone must have slandered Josef K., for one morning, without having done anything wrong, he was arrested."* (The Trial, Franz Kafka) – Immediate conflict:

Why was he arrested? Who accused him? What's going on?

- *"He was an old man who fished alone in a skiff in the Gulf Stream and he had gone eighty-four days now without taking a fish."* (The Old Man and the Sea, Ernest Hemingway) – The struggle is clear from the start—this is a man battling against the odds.

- *"My mother died today. Or maybe yesterday; I can't be sure."* (The Stranger, Albert Camus) – A disorienting, emotionless statement that creates immediate intrigue—why does the narrator feel this way?

How to apply this in your writing:

1. Open with a character facing a choice, dilemma, or unexpected event.
2. Establish stakes — what does the character stand to lose?
3. Use mystery — something feels off, and the reader wants to find out why.

3. Make It Impossible for Readers to Put Your Story Down.

Your opening hook should set the tone for the entire story and ensure readers are emotionally or intellectually hooked. To do this, create a sense of urgency or an emotional connection that makes readers *need* to find out what happens next. Whether it's through high-stakes action, a deeply personal moment, or a shocking revelation, your opening should build tension and momentum. It should give readers just enough to keep them coming back for more, leaving them with a sense that something important is about to unfold.

Ways to ensure your opening is unputdownable:

- **Create urgency** – ("We had six hours to get out of the city before they locked the gates forever.")

- **Establish an emotional connection** – A vulnerable or deeply personal moment can pull readers in emotionally. (Example: "When I was eight, my father left us for good. The last thing he said to me was, 'Be strong.' I still don't know what that means.")

- **Introduce a shocking or contradictory statement** – Something that challenges expectations makes the reader stop and think. (Example: "The last thing she expected on her wedding day was to be arrested.")

Examples of unforgettable opening hooks that demand attention:

- *"This is the saddest story I have ever heard."* (*The Good Soldier, Ford Madox Ford*) – Sets an emotional tone and foreshadows tragedy.

- *"The man in black fled across the desert, and the gunslinger followed."* (*The Dark Tower, Stephen King*) – Immediate tension: Who are these men? Why is one chasing the other?

- *"You better not never tell nobody but God."* (*The Color Purple, Alice Walker*) – Creates an immediate sense of secrecy, fear, and weighty stakes.

How to apply this in your writing:

1. End your first paragraph or scene with a reason to turn the page — a cliffhanger or unsettling question.

2. Establish a strong emotional or narrative voice — your opening should set the tone for the whole story.
3. Make readers feel like they've been dropped into something important — they need to keep reading to understand.

PART 9: MASTERING THE FINAL ELEMENTS OF YOUR STORY

This section dives into the elements that bring a story to life, from creating memorable villains and immersive world-building to using setting and atmosphere to enhance your narrative. You'll also explore how to craft a strong prologue that sets the stage and adapt your writing for different genres, equipping you with the skills to build rich, engaging stories that captivate readers.

TIP 41. HOW TO WRITE A MEMORABLE VILLAIN

A truly great villain is more than just an obstacle for the hero to overcome — they are often the driving force behind the plot, shaping the story just as much, if not more, than the protagonist. A well-crafted villain creates tension, raises stakes, and challenges the hero in profound ways, making the journey more engaging and emotionally charged.

The most iconic villains in literature and film aren't simply evil for the sake of being evil. They have depth, purpose, and their own sense of justice:

- **Darth Vader** (Star Wars) – A fallen Jedi driven by pain and manipulation, whose tragic past fuels his loyalty to the Emperor.

- **The Joker** (The Dark Knight) – A chaotic force of destruction who challenges Batman's sense of morality and order.

- **Cersei Lannister** (Game of Thrones) – A ruthless strategist whose fierce love for her family makes her actions, however cruel, deeply personal and understandable.

- **Killmonger** (Black Panther) – A villain whose motivations are rooted in real-world injustice, making him sympathetic even when his methods are brutal.

A villain should never feel like a caricature, instead, they should be as complex and compelling as your protagonist. Here's how to craft a villain who elevates your story, creates meaningful conflict, and lingers in the minds of your readers long after the final page.

1. Give Them a Believable Motivation for Their Actions.

A memorable villain doesn't act for the sake of being evil; they have a reason behind everything they do. Whether it's seeking revenge, a desire for power, or believing they're saving the world, their motivations should be clear and believable. The best villains often think they're the hero in their own story, and their actions should reflect their personal convictions. A villain who is driven by deep beliefs, past traumas, or a specific goal will feel more real and human. By understanding *why,* they do what they do, your readers will be able to empathize with them, even if they don't agree with their actions. A well-crafted motivation gives depth to the character and makes their actions feel justified, no matter how twisted.

Ways to develop strong motivations for your villain:

- **Personal vengeance** – They seek revenge for a past wrong (e.g., Count of Monte Cristo, Erik Killmonger).

- **Ideological beliefs** – They truly believe their actions serve a greater purpose (e.g., Thanos believes wiping out half the universe is an act of mercy).

- **Corruption through power** – They didn't start out evil, but ambition, fear, or manipulation changed them (e.g., Walter White in Breaking Bad).

- **Tragic past experiences** – Their past trauma influences their choices (e.g., Magneto's experience as a Holocaust survivor fuels his hatred for humans in X-Men).

- **The desire for control** – They believe order is the only way to prevent chaos (e.g., Dolores Umbridge in Harry Potter).

Examples of villains with compelling motivations:

- **Claude Frollo** (The Hunchback of Notre Dame) – His obsession with purity and sin leads him to commit terrible acts while convincing himself he is acting righteously.

- **The Wicked Witch of the West** (The Wizard of Oz) – In Wicked, she is reimagined as Elphaba, a misunderstood revolutionary fighting against an oppressive system.

- **Light Yagami** (Death Note) – A protagonist-turned-villain who starts with the goal of eliminating crime but becomes consumed by his own god complex.

How to apply this in your writing:

1. Ask: What does my villain want, and why do they believe they are justified?
2. Give them a personal backstory that explains their worldview.
3. Ensure that their actions are consistent with their beliefs, even if they are extreme.

2. Let Them Have Strengths as Well as Flaws.

A great villain isn't just a one-dimensional antagonist - they have strengths and weaknesses that make them multi-faceted. Maybe they're incredibly intelligent, resourceful, or charming, but they also have weaknesses, like arrogance, fear, or vulnerability. These traits make them feel more real and relatable, as no one is perfect, not even the villain. By giving your villain depth, you create a character that challenges the protagonist in meaningful ways, forcing them to confront their own flaws or weaknesses. A well-crafted villain is not just an unstoppable force — they are humanized by their weaknesses. Maybe they have a code of honor, a soft spot for someone, or an insecurity that ultimately leads to their downfall.

Examples of villains with strengths and flaws:

- **Hannibal Lecter** (The Silence of the Lambs) – Brilliant, cultured, and manipulative, yet his own monstrous nature isolates him.

- **Loki** (Thor, The Avengers) – A cunning trickster whose deep-seated insecurities drive his betrayals.

- **Miranda Priestly** (The Devil Wears Prada) – Fiercely intelligent and commanding, but her ruthless ambition costs her personal relationships.

How to apply this in your writing:

1. Make sure your villain's strengths challenge the protagonist — they should feel like a true threat.
2. Give them a weakness that makes them human and relatable.
3. Let their greatest flaw be the reason for their downfall — even if they are powerful, they should have blind spots that can be exploited.

3. Make Sure They Challenge Your Protagonist in Meaningful Ways.

The villain is at their most powerful when they challenge the protagonist on more than just a physical level. The best villains push your protagonist to grow and evolve, forcing them to face difficult choices, moral dilemmas, or emotional challenges. The villain's actions should shake the protagonist's beliefs, test their resolve, and create significant obstacles. Whether it's through ideological conflict, manipulation, or personal attacks, the villain should create stakes that make the hero's journey more meaningful. A villain who forces the protagonist to question their motivations, values, and even their identity adds complexity and depth to the entire narrative, making the hero's eventual victory more satisfying.

Ways a villain can challenge the protagonist:

- **Moral dilemmas** – The hero is forced to question their own beliefs or values because of the villain's actions. (Example: The Joker forces Batman to question his no-kill rule in The Dark Knight.)

- **Personal stakes** – The villain targets the hero's loved ones, making it more than just a fight—it's personal. (Example: Darth Vader being Luke's father raises the emotional stakes in Star Wars.)

- **Mirroring the protagonist** – The villain and hero have similar origins but took different paths. (Example: Erik Killmonger and T'Challa both want to help their people, but Killmonger uses violence while T'Challa seeks diplomacy.)

- **Forcing the hero to confront their fears** – The villain exposes the hero's weaknesses and forces them to overcome personal struggles. (Example: Pennywise in IT embodies the fears of each character, making their battle as much psychological as it is physical.)

Examples of villains who deeply challenge the protagonist:

- **Hans Landa** (Inglourious Basterds) – His intelligence and charm make him terrifying, forcing the protagonists into a constant psychological battle.

- **Professor Moriarty** (Sherlock Holmes) – A villain who is Holmes' intellectual equal, pushing him to his limits in a game of wits.

- **Voldemort** (Harry Potter) – More than just a powerful enemy, he represents the darkest path Harry could have taken, mirroring him in many ways.

How to apply this in your writing:

1. Ask: How does my villain force the hero to grow or change?
2. Make sure the villain isn't just a final obstacle — they should challenge the protagonist at every step.
3. Have the hero struggle with the villain's ideology or actions, making their victory more meaningful.

TIP 42. HOW TO BUILD WORLD-BUILDING IN FICTION

World-building is the foundation of believability and immersion in fiction. Whether you're writing fantasy, sci-fi, historical fiction, or even a richly detailed contemporary setting, your world should feel like a living, breathing place that influences your characters and story.

A well-built world does more than just provide a backdrop, it shapes culture, fuels conflicts, and impacts character choices. The most immersive worlds in fiction — from J.R.R. Tolkien's Middle-earth to Frank Herbert's Arrakis in *Dune* — feel tangible because they follow their own internal logic, rules, and histories.

World-building should make readers feel like they're stepping into a fully realized world, where everything from geography to politics, economy, and cultural traditions shapes the way characters interact. Here's how to build a world that feels as real as the one we live in.

1. Define the Rules and Boundaries of Your World.

Every world — whether a magical kingdom, a futuristic dystopia, or a hidden underground society — operates by a set of rules and limitations. These rules help maintain consistency and prevent the world from feeling random or implausible.

Key areas to define in your world:

- **Geography & Environment** – What does the landscape look like? Are there towering mountains, endless deserts, floating islands? How does geography affect society, trade, warfare, and travel? (Example: The desert planet of Arrakis in Dune isn't just a setting—it shapes the economy, power struggles, and way of life for its people.)

- **Magic or Technology** – If magic exists, what are its limits? What does it cost to use? If advanced technology is part of your world, how does it shape daily life, warfare, or communication? (Example: In Harry Potter, magic has rules — spells require wands, certain magic is forbidden, and there are social hierarchies based on magical ability.)

- **Natural & Physical Laws** – Does time flow differently? Are there multiple suns or moons? How does gravity work? (Example: Interstellar explores worlds where time passes at different rates due to relativity, creating high-stakes scenarios that feel scientifically plausible.)

- **Societal Norms & Values** – What is considered normal, sacred, or taboo? Does your society value honor, loyalty, or conquest? (Example: In The Hunger Games, the Capitol thrives on excess while the districts suffer in poverty, highlighting stark social inequalities.)

Examples of worlds with strong internal logic:

- **Middle-earth** (The Lord of the Rings) – A world rich in history, languages, and cultures, with distinct races (elves, dwarves, humans) who each have their own traditions and beliefs.

- **Westeros** (Game of Thrones) – A world where geography dictates power, from the cold North with its direwolves to the warm, politically treacherous South.

- **The Cyberpunk Future** (Blade Runner, Neuromancer) – High-tech dystopias where corporations rule, cities are overpopulated, and morality is a grey area.

How to apply this in your writing:

1. Establish your world's rules early on and stick to them.

2. Ask: What makes my world different from our own? How do those differences impact daily life?
3. Ensure your world has logic and limitations. There should be things shouldn't happen just for convenience.

2. Show the Culture, Politics, and Economy Through Actions.

Instead of dumping pages of exposition about how your world works, show it through your characters' experiences, interactions, and conflicts.

Ways to integrate world-building naturally:

- **Use cultural habits and customs** – Show how people greet each other, what they eat, and what holidays they celebrate. (Example: The elaborate court manners in Pride and Prejudice reveal the rigid social hierarchy of Regency England.)

- **Reveal class and economic systems through conflict** – Is wealth concentrated in the hands of a few? How do different social classes interact? (Example: In Les Misérables, the struggles of the poor vs. the privileged drive the entire story.)

- **Introduce politics through power struggles** – Who holds power? What laws or traditions cause conflict? (Example: The political maneuvering in The Hunger Games shows the brutal control of the Capitol over the districts.)

- **Let history shape the present** – Wars, revolutions, and ancient rivalries should influence the world today. (Example: In The Witcher, tensions between elves, humans, and mages stem from a long history of oppression and rebellion.)

Examples of immersive cultural world-building:

- **Panem** (The Hunger Games) – The Capitol's luxurious excess and the districts' suffering are shown through everyday life, not just exposition.

- **The Floating City of Laputa** (Castle in the Sky) – A once-thriving technological utopia, now a deserted relic of a lost civilization, reflected in its architecture, myths, and remaining artifacts.

- **The Wizarding World** (Harry Potter) – From Diagon Alley's magical shops to Hogwarts' sorting ceremony, everyday interactions bring the magical society to life.

How to apply this in your writing:

1. Show your world's culture through traditions, architecture, and daily routines, not just lengthy descriptions.
2. Let the economy and politics influence the characters — how do they survive, work, or rebel?
3. Reveal historical conflicts subtly — legends, ruins, or ancient books can hint at a rich past.

3. Make the World an Extension of Your Characters' Struggles.

The world you build should feel like an integral part of your characters' journey, not just a backdrop. The struggles your characters face should be shaped by the world around them. For example, a character growing up in a war-torn society may have a very different set of challenges compared to one living in a utopian society. The environment, cultural expectations, and societal constraints should play a role in shaping the protagonist's desires, fears, and actions. When the world and the character's struggles are intertwined, it adds emotional depth and makes the setting feel more alive and meaningful.

Ways the world can shape your characters:

- **Environmental obstacles** – A world's climate or geography should present physical struggles (Example: In The Revenant, the frozen wilderness is as much an enemy as the people hunting the protagonist).

- **Social expectations and constraints** – What does society demand of your characters? Do they conform or rebel? (Example: Mulan must disguise herself as a man to fight, highlighting gender roles in ancient China.)

- **Moral dilemmas based on world rules** – If magic, AI, or time travel exist, how does it challenge ethical boundaries? (Example: In Westworld, the ability to create lifelike robots raises questions about free will and consciousness.)

- **Shifting power dynamics** – Who controls the world, and how does that affect the protagonist? (Example: The rigid caste system in Red Rising defines every aspect of society and the protagonist's place in it.)

Examples of worlds that deeply affect the protagonist's struggles:

- **Gilead** (The Handmaid's Tale) – A dystopian society where women's rights have been stripped away, shaping Offred's entire existence and survival.

- **The War-Torn World of The Road** – A father and son struggle to survive in a world devoid of hope, morality, and safety.

- **The High Society of Bridgerton** – The rigid expectations of status, reputation, and marriage dictate every move the characters make.

How to apply this in your writing:

1. Make sure the world directly influences the protagonist's struggles — it shouldn't just be a backdrop.
2. Let societal rules create real stakes and obstacles that shape character choices.
3. Use your setting to heighten tension and emotional stakes, making the world feel alive.

TIP 43. THE POWER OF SETTING: HOW TO CREATE ATMOSPHERE IN YOUR STORY

Setting is more than just a location, it's an active force that shapes the mood, deepens emotions, and even drives the plot. A well-crafted setting can make a moment feel tense, romantic, eerie, or hopeful, immersing readers so deeply in the world that they experience it alongside your characters.

Think about how some of the greatest books and films use setting to enhance storytelling:

- **The Overlook Hotel in The Shining** – The eerie, isolated hotel becomes a psychological battlefield, mirroring Jack's descent into madness.

- **Gothic mansions in Jane Eyre and Rebecca** – These eerie, sprawling estates reflect the isolation and emotional turmoil of the protagonists.

- **The scorching, desolate world of Mad Max: Fury Road** – A setting that isn't just harsh, but also a constant physical and psychological threat to its characters.

- **The rain-soaked, neon-lit dystopia of Blade Runner** – A futuristic world that mirrors the themes of isolation, identity, and the blurred lines between humanity and machine.

Your setting should do more than tell readers where the story takes place, it should enhance the mood, mirror character emotions, and influence events. Here's how to turn your setting into a powerful storytelling tool.

1. Choose a Setting that Reflects Your Character's Mood.

The setting should reflect the internal state of your character, adding an emotional layer to the scene. A character feeling isolated and defeated might walk through a cold, gray city with empty streets and dreary weather, amplifying their sense of loneliness. Alternatively, a character who's in love or full of hope might experience a vibrant sunset or a warm, bustling environment that mirrors their positive emotions. This connection between the setting and the character's mood deepens the reader's connection to both the character and the story. The environment becomes an extension of the emotional landscape, making the setting not just a place, but a reflection of the character's inner world.

Ways to connect setting to character emotions:

- **A stormy sea can reflect inner turmoil or rising tension.** (Example: In Frankenstein, the violent storms and icy landscapes mirror Victor's growing obsession and despair.)

- **A decaying city can represent lost dreams or despair.** (Example: In The Road, the bleak, ruined world reflects the protagonist's desperation and dwindling hope.)

- **A sunlit, bustling town can reflect warmth, nostalgia, or renewal.** (Example: In Call Me by Your Name, the golden Italian countryside reinforces the sensual and fleeting nature of summer romance.)

Examples of setting reflecting mood:

- **In Les Misérables**, the grimy streets of revolutionary Paris mirror the characters' struggles and the larger fight for justice and survival.

- **In The Revenant**, the unforgiving frozen wilderness is both a physical and psychological battlefield, mirroring Hugh Glass's fight for survival and revenge.

- **In The Great Gatsby**, Gatsby's extravagant mansion is bright and opulent, yet empty and lonely, symbolizing the illusion of his dream.

How to apply this in your writing:

1. Ask: How does my character feel in this scene? How can the setting reflect or contrast that?
2. Use weather, landscapes, and architecture to emphasize tone and emotion.
3. Let the environment reinforce the stakes. A horror story set in a bright, cheerful village would lessen its impact.

2. Use Sensory Details to Immerse Your Readers in the Environment.

To truly bring your setting to life, engage all your readers' senses. Instead of just describing the scenery, let them smell the rain on the pavement, hear the distant hum of city traffic, or feel the warmth of the sun on their skin. Sensory details help make the setting feel tangible and real, and they create a richer atmosphere. Describe the sounds, sights, textures, and even tastes of the environment. If your character is walking through a forest, let the rustling of leaves or the scent of pine trees draw readers in. These immersive details create a stronger emotional connection to the scene and make readers feel like they're living in the world you've created.

Ways to use sensory details effectively:

- **Sight** – Instead of saying "It was a dark alley," describe the flickering streetlights, the graffiti-covered walls, and the shifting shadows in the corners.

- **Sound** – A forest isn't just "quiet"—it has the distant hoot of an owl, the rustling of leaves, and the whisper of the wind through the trees.

- **Smell** – A setting comes alive through scent—the smoky aroma of a fire, the sharp tang of salt in the air, or the metallic scent of blood after a battle.

- **Touch** – What does the world feel like? The rough bark of a tree, the sting of icy rain, the gritty sand beneath bare feet.

- **Taste** – Can a setting be tasted? Absolutely. The sweetness of fresh strawberries in a summer market, the bitter coffee in a worn-down diner, or the sharp burn of whiskey in a smoky bar.

Examples of sensory-rich settings:

- **In Chernobyl** (TV series), the radiation itself is invisible, but the stench of burning graphite, the suffocating heat, and the eerie silence create an overwhelming sense of dread.

- **In Perfume: The Story of a Murderer**, scent is the driving force of the novel—every location is defined by its unique smells, making the setting feel intoxicatingly vivid.

- **In Atonement**, the heatwave during the summer of 1935 makes every moment feel heavy, hazy, and charged with tension.

How to apply this in your writing:

1. Engage at least three senses per scene to make the world feel real.
2. Use specific, vivid details rather than generic descriptions ("The air was thick with the scent of wet earth and gasoline" is stronger than "It smelled bad.").

3. Think about how your character would experience the setting. A detective might notice different details than a grieving widow.

3. Let the Setting Influence the Plot. Make It a Character in Itself!

The setting should play an active role in your story, not just serve as a background. Whether it's a crumbling mansion, a harsh desert, or a futuristic city, the environment should influence your character's actions, decisions, and the overall plot. The setting can introduce challenges, reveal secrets, or even symbolize key themes in your story. For example, a haunted house might be a literal and metaphorical representation of a character's past, forcing them to confront buried emotions or memories. Let the world shape the character's choices and experiences, and make sure that the environment feels like an integral part of the narrative.

Ways the setting can influence the story:

- **Introduce natural dangers** – A blizzard, a collapsing bridge, or a rising flood can force characters to adapt or fight for survival.

- **Shape power dynamics** – A futuristic city with strict social classes will define who holds power and who rebels.

- **Create isolation or urgency** – A locked-room mystery, a stranded spaceship, or a town with a dark secret can intensify tension.

- **Serve as a metaphor** – A decaying house can represent a decaying mind (Example: Miss Havisham's house in

Great Expectations is a physical manifestation of her frozen-in-time heartbreak.)

Examples of setting as an active force:

- **In No Country for Old Men**, the vast, empty desert of Texas creates a sense of lawlessness and isolation, mirroring the relentless nature of fate.

- **In The Lighthouse**, the confined, storm-ravaged island traps the characters in a psychological and physical nightmare.

- **In The Martian**, Mars isn't just a setting — it's an adversary that Mark Watney must out-think and battle for survival.

How to apply this in your writing:

1. Ask: Does my setting introduce conflict or influence my character's choices?
2. Think about how the world affects survival, politics, emotions, and relationships.
3. Make the setting evolve: a city under siege, a forest that darkens as the journey progresses, or a town that changes as secrets unravel.

TIP 44. HOW TO WRITE A PROLOGUE THAT SETS THE STAGE

A well-crafted prologue is like a doorway because it draws readers in, teases the bigger picture, and sets the tone for what's to come. While not every story needs a prologue, when used effectively, it creates intrigue, establishes key world-building elements, and immerses the reader in your narrative before the main story even begins.

A great prologue doesn't feel like an info dump or an unnecessary prelude. In fact, it feels essential, leaving readers hungry for more. Some of the most famous books and films use prologues to frame the story, introduce mystery, or set up major themes:

- **The opening of Romeo and Juliet** – The famous prologue tells us exactly what's going to happen, but it doesn't take away from the emotional impact, it enhances the tragic inevitability.

- **The prologue in The Name of the Wind** – A simple yet mysterious passage that sets up the world and main character without overwhelming readers with exposition.

- **The introduction of The Fellowship of the Ring (film)** – This epic, visually stunning prologue provides crucial backstory about the One Ring while keeping tension high.

A prologue should intrigue, not overwhelm. It should give just enough to spark curiosity and ground readers in the world without giving away too much. Here's how to craft a powerful prologue that grabs attention and sets the perfect stage for your story.

1. Give a Glimpse of What's to Come, but Don't Spoil It!

The prologue should offer a taste of the story without giving away too much. This could mean teasing an upcoming event, revealing a snippet of an important conversation, or showing a glimpse of a future conflict. However, it's important to maintain a sense of mystery, don't spoil the story's twists or key moments. Think of it like a trailer for a movie: it should be intriguing enough to spark curiosity but not reveal the entire plot. The goal is to make the reader want to keep reading to uncover what happens next.

Effective ways to tease the story without spoiling it:

- **Flash forward to a critical moment** – Show a snippet of an intense or emotional scene that happens later in the story. Example: In The Book Thief, the prologue is narrated by Death, who foreshadows major events without revealing too much detail.

- **Present a mystery** – Open with an event that raises more questions than answers. Example: Gone Girl begins with the protagonist describing the shape of his missing wife's head, creating immediate unease and curiosity.

- **Reveal a legend or prophecy** – A prophecy, myth, or ancient text can hint at the conflict to come. Example: The Mortal Instruments begins with an old story about angels and demons, foreshadowing the supernatural war ahead.

- **Show an important event from the past** – A backstory prologue can give insight into something that shaped the world or the protagonist. Example: A Game of Thrones opens with a White Walker attack beyond the Wall, immediately establishing danger before we meet the main characters.

Examples of intriguing prologues:

- **In The Maze Runner**, the prologue hints at the world's dystopian nature without explaining too much, making readers desperate to understand how things got that way.

- **In Jurassic Park**, the prologue features a worker being attacked by a dinosaur, teasing the story's central danger before we meet the protagonists.

- **In Red Queen**, the prologue sets up the social hierarchy of a world divided by blood color, introducing tension before the plot unfolds.

How to apply this in your writing:

1. Avoid explaining too much. Instead, focus on questions, mystery, or atmosphere rather than dumping backstory.
2. Use vivid, intriguing language. The prologue should be atmospheric and gripping, not just informative.
3. Ask yourself: Will this make the reader eager to turn the page? If not, rethink your approach.

2. Establish the World or Key Elements Early On.

The prologue is a great place to introduce the setting, the world's rules, or key elements that will be crucial later in the story. Whether it's a magical system, the political landscape, or the stakes of the story, give readers a sense of what's at play. If your story takes place in a fantasy world, your prologue could give a sneak peek of the world's magic or history. If your book is set in a dystopian society, introduce the tension of that world early on. This sets up expectations and allows the reader to feel grounded in the world before the main story begins.

What you can establish in the prologue:

- **The rules of the world** – Is it a futuristic society? A kingdom ruled by magic? A dystopia where people are divided by social class? Example: The prologue of The Giver subtly introduces the idea of a "perfect" world where emotions and memories are controlled.

- **The stakes** – What's at risk in this world? Who holds power? Example: The Night Circus begins with a simple but chilling statement: "The circus arrives without warning." This immediately sets the tone for an eerie, magical tale.

- **A past event that changed everything** – If your story is set in a post-apocalyptic world, the prologue could show the moment when everything fell apart. Example: The Road never explicitly tells us what destroyed the world, but the tone and setting in the opening pages establish a sense of desolation.

Examples of world-building prologues that work:

- **In The Hunger Games (film adaptation)**, the opening text explains the history of the districts and the games, setting up the world without overwhelming the viewer.

- **In The Lies of Locke Lamora**, the prologue introduces the world's crime culture and establishes the protagonist's unique upbringing.

- **In The Way of Kings**, the prologue shows a pivotal moment in history — a betrayal that shapes the entire world, giving readers a foundation to understand the current events.

How to apply this in your writing:

1. Focus on only what the reader absolutely needs to know. Don't overload them with details.
2. Use engaging imagery, action, or dialogue instead of pure explanation.
3. Make sure the tone of the prologue matches the rest of the story — it should feel like part of the same book, not a separate info dump.

3. Make It Compelling Enough that Readers Can't Wait to Dive into the Main Story!

The prologue should be engaging and exciting enough that readers are hooked immediately. Whether it's through a compelling mystery, an action-packed scene, or an emotionally charged moment, the prologue should make the reader want to know more. It should act as a hook that draws readers in, making them eager to continue reading. The opening of your story should have a sense of urgency or intrigue, creating a seamless transition to the main plot.

Ways to make your prologue compelling:

- **Open with high stakes** – Start with a conflict, an action scene, or an intense emotional moment. Example: The Girl with the Dragon Tattoo begins with an old man receiving a mysterious package related to an unsolved crime, immediately drawing readers into the mystery.

- **Use a strong, unique voice** – The prologue should feel immersive and immediate, not distant and detached. Example: The Name of the Wind uses poetic, rhythmic prose to make the opening lines unforgettable.

- **Create a sense of urgency** – Readers should feel like they need to keep reading. Example: The Road begins with the father waking up and checking if his son is still breathing, instantly creating tension and emotional stakes.

Examples of gripping prologues:

- **In Divergent**, the prologue briefly introduces the faction system, making readers curious about how this society works.

- **In Cinder**, the prologue hints at a futuristic plague and a hidden secret, instantly setting up intrigue.

- **In Shadow and Bone**, the prologue shows a childhood event that foreshadows the protagonist's destiny, making it feel essential to the story.

How to apply this in your writing:

1. Make sure your prologue raises compelling questions, leaving the readers wanting answers.
2. Don't make it too long. A prologue should be concise and impactful.
3. Ensure that the transition into Chapter 1 feels seamless, not like a completely different story.

TIP 45. WRITING FOR DIFFERENT GENRES: TIPS FOR EVERY TYPE OF WRITER

Every genre has its own rules, themes, and expectations, and to master writing in a specific genre, you need to understand what makes it work. Readers gravitate toward genres because they expect certain elements — a detective solving a crime in mystery, an epic battle of good vs. evil in fantasy, or a heart-wrenching emotional arc in romance.

But while knowing the conventions is essential, mastering a genre also means knowing when to break the rules, subvert tropes, and add your own unique voice. Some of the most celebrated books and films follow genre expectations while pushing boundaries:

- **Mystery: Big Little Lies** by Liane Moriarty blends a murder mystery with contemporary drama, focusing on relationships and social issues as much as solving the crime.

- **Fantasy: Circe** by Madeline Miller takes a well-known Greek myth and tells it from a feminine, character-driven perspective, challenging the typical action-heavy fantasy narrative.

- **Science Fiction: The Three-Body Problem** by Liu Cixin takes a hard science approach, prioritizing physics and philosophical questions over traditional action-driven sci-fi.

- **Horror: The Haunting of Hill House** by Shirley Jackson proves that horror doesn't have to be about gore— psychological tension and eerie atmospheres can be just as terrifying.

- **Historical Fiction: The Nightingale** by Kristin Hannah shifts the focus from epic battles to the untold stories of women in war, adding an emotional depth often missing in war fiction.

Understanding a genre doesn't mean you have to write predictably. It means knowing how to meet reader expectations while finding ways to innovate. Here's how to master genre writing without losing your unique voice.

1. Know the Conventions of the Genre You're Writing In.

Every genre has its own established rules, tropes, and expectations. For example, a romance novel typically involves a love story with a happy ending, while a mystery relies on puzzles, clues, and a dramatic reveal. Understanding these conventions is key to crafting a story that resonates with readers who are looking for what's familiar within that genre. This doesn't mean you have to follow the formula to a T, but you should be aware of the genre's key elements, such as character arcs, plot structure, and themes. Whether it's the hero's journey in fantasy or the suspenseful buildup in a thriller, make sure you know what readers expect - and then consider how you can creatively twist or play with those conventions.

Key conventions of different genres:

- **Mystery:** A crime, a detective (or amateur sleuth), red herrings, a slow reveal of clues, and a final twist. *Example: Agatha Christie's Murder on the Orient Express plays with classic detective novel expectations but subverts them with its shocking ending.

- **Fantasy:** A rich, immersive world, magic or supernatural elements, a hero's journey, and a battle between forces of good and evil. Example: The Lord of the Rings follows the hero's journey but adds deep mythology and world-building.

- **Science Fiction:** Advanced technology, futuristic settings, scientific exploration, and questions about society, ethics, and humanity. Example: Dune blends political intrigue, environmental themes, and religious undertones within a sci-fi setting.

- **Romance:** A central love story, emotional depth, relationship conflicts, and a satisfying resolution. Example: Pride and Prejudice set the template for romantic tension, misunderstandings, and ultimate reconciliation.

- **Thriller/Suspense:** High stakes, an urgent or deadly situation, short and intense chapters, and plot twists. Example: The Silence of the Lambs masterfully builds psychological suspense, using pacing to keep tension high.

Examples of authors who bend genre conventions:

- **Margaret Atwood (The Handmaid's Tale)** – A dystopian novel with the intimate, personal narration of literary fiction, making it feel terrifyingly real.

- **Kazuo Ishiguro (Never Let Me Go)** – A sci-fi novel that feels more like a quiet, introspective drama, proving that science fiction can be subtle and poetic.

- **Colson Whitehead (The Underground Railroad)** – A historical novel that introduces elements of magical realism, reimagining the Underground Railroad as an actual railway system.

How to apply this in your writing:

1. Research successful books in your genre and analyze how they handle structure, pacing, and character arcs.
2. Consider how your story fits into the genre and where it might break the mold.
3. Ask yourself: What do readers expect from this genre, and how can I both meet and surprise them?

2. Adjust Pacing to Match Genre Expectations.

Different genres have different pacing requirements. In romance, the pacing may be slower and more focused on emotional depth, while in thrillers, you'll need quick, heart-pounding moments to keep readers on the edge of their seat. Fantasy novels might have a slower build-up to establish the world, while in science fiction, you may need to balance world-building with action to keep the plot moving forward. Understanding the pacing expectations of the genre you're working in ensures that your story doesn't feel sluggish or rushed. Fast-paced genres require tension, short scenes, and escalating stakes, while slower genres may focus on introspection, character relationships, or setting the atmosphere.

How pacing differs across genres:

- **Thrillers & Mysteries:** Short, punchy chapters, cliffhangers, and constant tension. Example: The Girl with the Dragon Tattoo keeps chapters short, often ending with a revelation that forces the reader to keep going.

- **Fantasy & Science Fiction:** Slower buildup with detailed world-building, punctuated by action or revelations.

Example: The Hobbit starts leisurely but quickens its pace as Bilbo's journey intensifies.

- **Romance:** Steady, emotional pacing, allowing readers to invest deeply in the characters' relationship. Example: Me Before You by Jojo Moyes builds emotional stakes gradually, making the climax hit harder.

- **Literary Fiction:** Often slower, more reflective, focusing on inner conflict rather than external action. Example: The Goldfinch by Donna Tartt spends entire sections inside the protagonist's thoughts, unravelling his past and emotions.

Examples of pacing used effectively:

- **Stephen King (The Shining)** – Uses slow, creeping dread before explosive moments of horror.

- **Suzanne Collins (The Hunger Games)** – Fast-paced, urgent action keeps the stakes high.

- **Emily Brontë (Wuthering Heights)** – Lingers on emotions and relationships, allowing gothic tension to build slowly.

How to apply this in your writing:

1. Determine the ideal pace for your story—does it need tension and speed, or deep introspection?
2. Use shorter sentences and paragraphs in fast-paced genres to heighten urgency.
3. Balance slow world-building with moments of action in fantasy and sci-fi to keep readers engaged.

3. Stay True to Your Voice While Respecting the Genre's Rules.

While it's important to adhere to the conventions of the genre, your unique voice should always shine through. Readers can tell when a writer is trying too hard to fit into a specific mold, so don't be afraid to infuse your style, tone, and perspective into your work. For example, even in a classic mystery, your character's voice, humor, and worldview can make the story feel fresh and new. Balancing your voice with genre expectations is the sweet spot where you can truly shine as a writer. Just because you're writing in a specific genre doesn't mean you have to give up your authenticity, make sure to embrace the genre's framework, while also letting your personal style breathe life into the story.

Ways to balance originality with genre expectations:

- **Infuse your personal style into dialogue and narration.** Example: Neil Gaiman writes fantasy, but his humorous, poetic voice makes his books feel uniquely his own.

- **Twist a common trope into something new.** Example: The Twilight series took the well-known vampire myth and added a romantic YA twist.

- **Experiment with format and storytelling techniques.** Example: Daisy Jones & The Six by Taylor Jenkins Reid is structured as an oral history, making it stand out among other music dramas.

Examples of genre fiction with strong authorial voice:

- **Gabriel García Márquez (One Hundred Years of Solitude)** – A blend of historical fiction and magical realism, written in his signature lyrical style.

- **Ray Bradbury (Fahrenheit 451)** – A dystopian sci-fi novel, but written with poetic, evocative prose.
- **Toni Morrison (Beloved)** – A ghost story wrapped in literary fiction, exploring trauma and history through haunting imagery.

How to apply this in your writing:

1. Don't try to mimic other authors. Let your natural voice shape the story.
2. Think about what excites you about the genre and lean into that passion.
3. Ask: How can I add a unique twist without straying too far from what readers love?

PART 10: PERFECTING YOUR CRAFT AND MOVING FORWARD

This section explores the key elements that make a story emotionally powerful and unforgettable. From building an emotional story arc and mastering foreshadowing to writing complex female characters, controlling pacing, and crafting narratives that truly resonate with readers, these final insights will help you create stories that connect deeply, linger in the mind, and stand the test of time.

TIP 46. HOW TO WRITE AN EMOTIONAL STORY ARC

An emotional story arc is what keeps readers connected to your characters. It's the reason they care about what happens, why they root for your protagonist, and why they feel invested in the journey. A strong emotional arc is more than just a character going through events; it's about internal transformation, growth, and change.

In some of the most powerful books, films, and TV shows, emotional arcs are what leave a lasting impact on audiences:

- **Frodo Baggins (The Lord of the Rings)** – His journey isn't just about destroying the One Ring; it's about his inner battle with power, corruption, and his loss of innocence.

- **Walter White (Breaking Bad)** – An emotional arc can also be a descent rather than growth. Walter's transformation from a desperate, well-meaning teacher to a ruthless drug lord is just as compelling as any redemptive arc.

- **Elizabeth Bennet (Pride and Prejudice)** – She begins with pride in her judgment and prejudice against others, but through experience and self-reflection, she learns to see beyond first impressions.

- **Simba (The Lion King)** – He must overcome guilt and self-doubt to step into his role as king, showing that emotional arcs often revolve around a character accepting responsibility.

A character's emotional evolution should be just as impactful as the external events in the story. Here's how to craft an emotional arc that feels real, relatable, and deeply moving.

1. Start with Your Character's Flaws and Struggles.

Every emotional arc begins with a character who has something they need to overcome, whether it's an internal conflict, a personal flaw, or a difficult situation they're facing. These struggles could be fear, self-doubt, guilt, or something more specific, like a traumatic event or a toxic relationship. To make the emotional journey relatable, begin with something that feels real and universal, even if it's unique to your character. The struggles at the start of the story should shape their motivations and set the stage for growth. Readers need to understand what's holding the character back emotionally so they can cheer them on as they work toward change.

Ways to establish a character's emotional struggle:

- **Internal Conflict:** What is the character struggling with within themselves?

    Example: Tony Stark in Iron Man starts off as arrogant and selfish, only to be forced into a situation where he must reconsider his values.

- **Emotional Wound:** What past event shaped their mindset or fears?

    Example: Katniss Everdeen (The Hunger Games) suffers from severe trauma and survival guilt, which affects her ability to trust others.

- **Fear or Self-Doubt:** What belief is holding them back?

    Example: Miles Morales (Spider-Man: Into the Spider-Verse) doesn't believe he's good enough to be a hero, which makes his eventual transformation powerful.

- **Unresolved Grief or Guilt:** Is there something in their past they can't let go of?

    Example: Joel (The Last of Us) is haunted by his daughter's death, making his emotional arc about learning to love and protect again.

Examples of characters with strong initial flaws or struggles:

- **Luke Skywalker (*Star Wars*)** – Begins naïve and full of self-doubt, unsure if he has what it takes to become a Jedi.

- **Moana (*Moana*)** – Struggles with duty vs. personal desire, feeling torn between staying in her village and following her adventurous spirit.

- **Bojack Horseman (*Bojack Horseman*)** – A character who masks deep self-loathing with humor and detachment, showing that emotional arcs can be about learning to break self-destructive patterns.

How to apply this in your writing:

1. Ask: *What is my character's biggest emotional struggle at the start?*
2. Make sure their flaw directly affects their actions and decisions in the beginning.

3. Let the reader understand why they struggle with this flaw through backstory, relationships, or their worldview.

2. Build Their Emotional Journey Through Highs and Lows.

An emotional story arc isn't just a straight line to happiness. It's a journey filled with ups and downs, victories and setbacks. As your character faces challenges and moments of triumph, their emotional state should fluctuate, making the journey feel authentic and unpredictable. After moments of growth or success, there should be struggles or moments of doubt that threaten to undo the character's progress. These emotional highs and lows create tension and keep readers emotionally engaged. Whether the character faces a personal setback, a loss, or a new revelation, each moment should move them closer to their ultimate transformation, while maintaining the tension of their emotional journey.

Ways to create an engaging emotional journey:

- **Moments of Growth:** Show the character taking a step forward.

  Example: Rocky (Rocky) starts training harder, believing in himself after struggling with self-worth.

- **Setbacks and Relapses:** Let them fall back into old habits or doubt themselves.

  Example: Elsa (Frozen) tries to embrace her powers but still isolates herself when fear takes over.

- **Turning Points:** A revelation or event forces them to change their perspective.

    Example: Andy (Toy Story 3) realizing it's time to let go of his childhood toys, bringing emotional closure.

- **Emotional Tension in Relationships:** Show how their struggles affect those around them.

    Example: In The Fault in Our Stars, Hazel and Augustus' relationship is bittersweet because of the inevitable pain it will bring, deepening their emotional arc.

Examples of characters with powerful emotional highs and lows:

- **Maximus (Gladiator)** – He starts as a loyal general, loses everything, fights as a slave, and ultimately regains his honor in death.

- **Beth Harmon (The Queen's Gambit)** – She struggles with addiction, trauma, and self-doubt, only to find strength in the people who care for her.

- **Will Hunting (Good Will Hunting)** – His arc isn't just about intelligence, it's about learning to open up and accept love and help from others.

How to apply this in your writing:

1. Ask: How does my character struggle with change?
2. Show emotional setbacks to keep tension high.
3. Let the journey feel messy and real. Remember, growth doesn't happen overnight.

3. End with Growth, Change, or Resolution. Emotions are Everything.

The emotional arc should culminate in a satisfying conclusion where the character either grows emotionally, achieves a resolution to their inner conflict, or learns to accept or overcome their struggles. This growth could be seen in the way they handle challenges, the new strength they've found, or the relationships they've built. The emotional journey should come full circle, offering readers a sense of closure or transformation. Whether it's through overcoming a fear, learning to love themselves, or reconciling with someone from their past, the emotional payoff should feel earned and meaningful. This resolution is the emotional heart of the story and should leave readers feeling moved, satisfied, or reflective.

Ways to end an emotional arc effectively:

- **Acceptance of Change:** The character learns a lesson that allows them to move forward.

    Example: Marlin (Finding Nemo) learns to let go and trust his son, completing his arc of overprotectiveness.

- **Healing or Overcoming a Fear:** The character faces their greatest fear and comes out stronger.

    Example: In Inside Out, Joy realizes that sadness is an essential part of life, leading to a touching emotional resolution.

- **A Bittersweet Conclusion:** Not all endings are happy, but they should feel meaningful.

Example: In Titanic, Rose's final act of letting go of Jack's memory represents her emotional growth and newfound independence.

- **A Sacrificial or Transformative Ending:** The character gives up something important but gains something greater.

  Example: In Schindler's List, Oskar Schindler realizes too late that he could have saved more lives, an emotionally devastating but powerful conclusion.

Examples of powerful emotional resolutions:

- **Jean Valjean (Les Misérables)** – A man who learns redemption through selflessness, ending his journey at peace.
- **Tony Stark (Avengers: Endgame)** – His arc comes full circle as he sacrifices himself for the greater good, completing his transition from selfish playboy to ultimate hero.
- **Rick Blaine (Casablanca)** – He starts cynical and self-serving but chooses to let Ilsa go for the greater good, proving he has changed.

How to apply this in your writing:

1. Ask: What lesson has my character learned by the end?
2. Ensure the final moment ties back to the beginning, showing how they've changed.
3. Make the emotional payoff feel earned. It should feel like the character worked for it, suffered for it, and ultimately embraced it.

TIP 47. THE ART OF FORESHADOWING: PLANTING CLUES FOR YOUR READERS

Foreshadowing is one of the most powerful storytelling techniques, allowing writers to plant seeds early that pay off later in a way that feels both surprising and inevitable. When done effectively, foreshadowing creates tension, builds intrigue, and deepens the reader's engagement by giving them subtle clues about future events.

The best stories across literature, television, and film masterfully use foreshadowing to enhance storytelling:

- **The Godfather (1972)** – During Michael Corleone's first scene, he tells Kay, "That's my family, Kay, not me." This moment subtly hints at his eventual transformation into the ruthless leader of the Corleone family.

- **Breaking Bad (2008-2013)** – The opening of each season often includes cryptic black-and-white flash-forwards, teasing future disasters while leaving viewers questioning how things will unfold.

- **1984** by George Orwell – The novel repeatedly hints at Winston's inevitable downfall, from O'Brien's early interactions to the ominous warnings about Big Brother always watching.

Foreshadowing doesn't just hint at future events, it strengthens the emotional impact of your story's climax. Here's how to use it effectively in your writing.

1. Drop Subtle Hints Early that Allude to Future Events.

Foreshadowing is most effective when it's woven subtly into the early parts of the story. These hints can take many forms: a seemingly casual remark, an object that seems out of place, or a piece of dialogue that might not make sense at first. The key is to keep these clues light and vague, giving the reader just enough to spark curiosity. These early hints should pique interest but not give away too much. For example, mentioning a character's recurring dream early in the story might seem insignificant at first, but it can later tie into an important plot twist or revelation. These seemingly small details will later prove meaningful, adding layers to the narrative.

Ways to foreshadow subtly:

- **Dialogue** – A seemingly offhand remark that takes on new meaning later.

    Example: In The Dark Knight (2008), Harvey Dent says, "You either die a hero or live long enough to see yourself become the villain." This line foreshadows his tragic transformation into Two-Face.

- **Objects and Symbols** – A recurring object or setting that gains importance as the story progresses.

    Example: In Citizen Kane (1941), the word "Rosebud" is referenced multiple times before its significance is revealed, giving the film a sense of lingering mystery.

- **Recurring Imagery** – Visual motifs or descriptions that hint at underlying themes.

Example: In No Country for Old Men (2007), the frequent imagery of fate and chance subtly foreshadows the unpredictable violence to come.

- **Unusual Behavior or Statements** – A character acting slightly off or making an unusual comment can be a subtle way to hint at the future.

  Example: In Fight Club (1999), Tyler Durden tells the narrator, "If you wake up at a different time, in a different place, could you wake up as a different person?" This seemingly casual remark foreshadows the narrator's identity twist.

Examples of foreshadowing through subtle hints:

- **In The Prestige (2006)**, Tesla warns Angier that his machine will bring him nothing but misery, foreshadowing the horrifying truth of how it works.
- **In The Sixth Sense (1999)**, Malcolm never interacts directly with people other than Cole, subtly hinting at the movie's twist.
- **In Blood Meridian** by Cormac McCarthy, the Judge's philosophical speeches about survival and dominance hint at the brutal and inevitable final confrontation.

How to apply this in your writing:

1. Ask: What's one key event I want to foreshadow? How can I hint at it subtly early on?
2. Use throwaway details that gain importance later.
3. Introduce a symbol, phrase, or minor event that will later connect to a major plot development.

2. Make Sure the Foreshadowing Doesn't Give Too Much Away.

The best foreshadowing is subtle. If you give away too much too soon, you risk ruining the surprise or tension when the event finally occurs. Foreshadowing should raise questions without answering them immediately. Readers should be able to look back after the event happens and think, "Ah, that makes sense now!" If foreshadowing is too obvious, it can feel heavy-handed and spoil the surprise. Let the hints create a sense of mystery that builds over time, so when the foreshadowed event finally unfolds, it feels both surprising and inevitable.

How to balance foreshadowing without over-explaining:

- **Use misdirection** – Lead the audience to suspect one thing, then reveal something else.

  Example: In Parasite (2019), the old housekeeper's odd behavior foreshadows a shocking secret but doesn't make it obvious until the moment of revelation.

- **Give multiple possible interpretations** – A hint should raise questions, not answer them.

  Example: In The Silence of the Lambs (1991), Hannibal Lecter's cryptic clue "Look deep within yourself" initially seems like a philosophical remark, but it's actually a direct hint about Buffalo Bill's identity.

- **Make the clue seem unimportant at first** – Readers shouldn't immediately recognize it as significant.

Example: In Pulp Fiction (1994), Vincent casually warns Butch about the dangers of a gold watch, foreshadowing how it will lead to a violent confrontation.

- **Spread hints over multiple scenes** – Rather than foreshadowing everything at once, drop small hints throughout the story.

    Example: In The Green Mile (1999), Coffey's healing abilities are revealed gradually, making his final act feel both unexpected and inevitable.

Examples of foreshadowing done subtly without giving too much away:

- **In 12 Angry Men (1957)**, the use of shadow and light foreshadows which jurors will change their stance as the film progresses.

- **In Requiem for a Dream (2000)**, early conversations about "the big score" foreshadow the eventual tragic downfall of each character.

- **In Atonement** by Ian McEwan, small shifts in perspective foreshadow the devastating truth revealed at the end.

How to apply this in your writing:

1. Avoid on-the-nose foreshadowing. Make it subtle enough that readers don't immediately recognize it.
2. Let foreshadowing add intrigue rather than outright answering a question.
3. Think about how to make your reveal surprising, yet logical in hindsight.

3. Tie the Foreshadowing Back to the Plot in a Satisfying Way.

Foreshadowing isn't just about dropping hints, it's about paying them off in a way that feels earned. As the story progresses, these earlier clues should come to fruition in a way that surprises and satisfies the reader. This payoff should feel natural, as though everything that has come before is leading to this moment. For instance, a minor detail introduced early on, such as an old map or a cryptic letter, should play a key role in the resolution of the plot, tying everything together in a way that makes the foreshadowing feel purposeful. This creates a sense of cohesion in the story and rewards attentive readers.

Ways to make the payoff satisfying:

- **Ensure the clue plays a major role later** – If you hint at something, make sure it matters in the resolution.

    Example: In The Usual Suspects (1995), the seemingly random details Verbal Kint shares early on turn out to be pieces of an elaborate lie that lead to the shocking reveal.

- **Reveal the significance of an earlier moment** – Let readers rethink previous scenes in a new light.

    Example: In Memento (2000), moments that seemed insignificant at first become crucial once the audience understands the protagonist's condition.

- **Make it feel inevitable** – The best foreshadowing turns what could have been a surprise into an inevitability.

Example: In Schindler's List (1993), Schindler's early motivations seem purely financial, but small hints throughout the film foreshadow his ultimate transformation.

Examples of satisfying foreshadowing payoffs:

- **In The Prestige**, Borden's line "Are you watching closely?" gains significance once his secret is revealed.

- **In No Country for Old Men**, Anton Chigurh's repeated use of a coin toss subtly foreshadows the film's final scene.

- **In One Flew Over the Cuckoo's Nest**, McMurphy's talk of freedom takes on a chilling new meaning by the end.

How to apply this in your writing:

1. Ask: Does my foreshadowing lead to a satisfying payoff?
2. Ensure the hint feels meaningful once the big moment arrives.
3. Reward attentive readers with details they can look back on and connect.

TIP 48. WRITING STRONG FEMALE CHARACTERS: HOW TO MAKE THEM COMPLEX AND REAL

A truly strong female character isn't just physically tough, hyper-independent, or "not like other girls", she's a fully realized, multi-dimensional person with her own motivations, flaws, strengths, and emotional depth. Strength doesn't always mean being fearless or dominant, it can be found in vulnerability, intelligence, emotional resilience, or the ability to make difficult choices.

Some of the most iconic female characters in literature, film, and television have left lasting impressions because they were written as complex individuals, rather than stereotypes:

- **Clarice Starling** (The Silence of the Lambs) – A brilliant and driven FBI trainee, whose intelligence and resilience allow her to stand her ground in a male-dominated field, yet she still struggles with fear, self-doubt, and trauma.

- **Ellen Ripley (Alien)** – One of the best examples of a female protagonist who takes charge, thinks strategically, and isn't defined by romance or her relationships—she's simply the best person for survival.

- **Jo March (Little Women)** – A headstrong and ambitious woman who defies societal norms, but still struggles with self-doubt, family expectations, and the push-pull between her personal dreams and responsibilities.

- **Celie (The Color Purple)** – A deeply complex character who survives immense trauma and oppression, yet finds her own strength, self-worth, and voice over time.

A strong female character is simply a well-written character. She should drive the story forward, have her own motivations, and feel as real as any male lead. Here's how to create female characters who are complex, compelling, and memorable.

1. Give Them Depth - Flaws and Strengths Alike.

A strong female character is one who is well-rounded and has a balance of both strengths and flaws. Just like any character, she should have a complex inner world, filled with insecurities, fears, and desires, alongside her abilities, courage, and intelligence. If she's only defined by her strengths, she risks becoming a one-dimensional "ideal," which can be less relatable. Perhaps she's fiercely independent but struggles with trust, or maybe she's resourceful but sometimes overthinks decisions. These imperfections are what make her real and engaging. A character's flaws are as important as their strengths because they contribute to their growth throughout the story. A character who has room to evolve is always more compelling.

How to create a well-rounded female character:

- **Give her a defining strength that sets her apart** – Intelligence, determination, resilience, or resourcefulness.

   Example: Lisbeth Salander (The Girl with the Dragon Tattoo) is a genius hacker with an unmatched intellect, but she also struggles with trust and social isolation.

- **Make her imperfect — give her weaknesses or fears** – She should struggle with something real, whether it's emotional vulnerability, self-doubt, or past trauma.

   Example: In A Streetcar Named Desire, Blanche DuBois is intelligent and refined, but her dependence on fantasy and alcohol leads to her downfall.

- **Show her evolution through her choices** – Her flaws should be part of her journey, not just set dressing.

Example: In Gone with the Wind, Scarlett O'Hara starts as selfish and manipulative, but by the end, her experiences force her to grow into a survivor who learns from her mistakes.

Examples of flawed but compelling female leads:

- **Marge Gunderson (Fargo)** – A sharp and compassionate police officer, balancing her investigative brilliance with her deeply human warmth.

- **Sophie Zawistowski (Sophie's Choice)** – A woman whose past haunts her, and whose ultimate flaw isn't weakness, but unbearable guilt and trauma.

- **The Bride (Kill Bill)** – A character driven by vengeance, yet not immune to pain, grief, and a longing for a lost life.

How to apply this in your writing:

1. Ask: What are my character's biggest strengths? What are her biggest weaknesses?
2. Make sure her strengths don't make her invincible. They should come with emotional or personal costs.
3. Let her grow over time by overcoming, or coming to terms with, her flaws.

2. Make Their Decisions Impactful and Their Actions Purposeful.

Strong female characters don't just react to events, they make decisions that push the plot forward. Whether it's choosing between personal sacrifice and achieving a greater good, standing up for what they believe in, or taking risks to protect someone they love, their choices should have weight. These decisions shouldn't be dictated by others but should come from a place of personal agency. Her actions need to feel purposeful, whether she's overcoming an obstacle, fighting for a cause, or choosing a difficult path. The direction she takes in the story should influence the outcome and make her arc feel earned. Readers should feel that her actions are motivated by her goals, experiences, and beliefs, not just a plot device.

How to make sure your female character has agency:

- **Give her a defining goal that fuels her actions** – She should have clear motivations that push the plot forward.

  Example: In Mad Max: Fury Road, Furiosa isn't just a side character — she's the true protagonist, leading the charge toward revolution and freedom.

- **Let her make bold choices, even if they come with consequences** – She shouldn't just follow others' paths but actively shape her own fate.

  Example: In Gone Girl, Amy Dunne's choices are extreme and controversial, but she remains a fully realized character, making decisions that alter the course of the story.

- **Showcase her problem-solving skills and resilience** – She doesn't need to be fearless, but she should be resourceful and capable.

  Example: In The Girl on the Train, Rachel Watson is unreliable and struggling with addiction, but her relentless search for the truth ultimately drives the entire plot.

Examples of female leads who make meaningful choices:

- **Sarah Connor (Terminator 2: Judgment Day)** – Transforms from a frightened woman into a fierce warrior, making tough choices for the sake of humanity.

- **Nora Helmer (A Doll's House)** – Chooses self-liberation over societal expectations, a groundbreaking act of independence for literature at the time.

- **Sethe (Beloved)** – Her past choices define the emotional heart of the story, and she must confront them to find healing.

How to apply this in your writing:

1. Ask: Does my female character make real decisions, or does she just react to others?
2. Ensure that her choices directly impact the plot's outcome.
3. Don't let her fall into passive roles. Instead, make her shape her own fate.

3. Let Them Have Their Own Goals, Separate from Their Relationships.

While relationships (romantic, familial, or platonic) can play a significant role in shaping a female character, her motivations and desires should be her own. Too often, female characters are written in terms of their relationships with others (i.e., as a lover, mother, or friend). A strong female character has her own goals, ambitions, and needs, which stand apart from how she is defined by the people around her. Whether she's striving for a career goal, seeking self-empowerment, or pursuing a dream, let her story center on what *she* wants, not just how others perceive her. This gives her autonomy and ensures her character is fully realized as a unique individual.

How to make sure she's defined by more than romance or family:

- **Give her a personal dream or ambition** – Something that drives her beyond relationships.

   Example: In The Piano, Ada McGrath's passion for music is central to her identity, more than any romance.

- **Make her relationships complex, but not her only focus** – Her emotional growth should not depend entirely on love.

   Example: In Three Billboards Outside Ebbing, Missouri, Mildred's grief and determination to find justice define her character more than any romantic subplot.

- **Show her independence and autonomy** – She should have a clear sense of self.

   Example: In The Color Purple, Celie's story is about her journey toward self-love and independence, not just romantic fulfillment.

Examples of female leads with strong independent arcs:

- **Frances McDormand (Nomadland)** – A woman choosing a transient life on her own terms, driven by personal freedom, not societal expectations.

- **Mildred Hayes (Three Billboards Outside Ebbing, Missouri)** – Fights for justice on her own terms, refusing to be sidelined by men around her.

- **Jo March (Little Women)** – Wants to be a writer first and foremost, rejecting the idea that marriage is her only purpose.

How to apply this in your writing:

1. Ask: What does my female character want for herself?
2. Avoid making her entire personality revolve around a love story.
3. Ensure that her narrative arc exists beyond just who she loves or helps.

TIP 49. THE IMPORTANCE OF PACING IN YOUR STORY

Pacing is the rhythm of storytelling, shaping how readers experience tension, emotion, and action. A well-paced story flows naturally, keeping the reader engaged without feeling rushed or sluggish. Too fast, and emotional moments get lost; too slow, and the story drags. Mastering pacing means knowing when to speed up and when to slow down. It's the difference between a book readers devour in one sitting and one they put down halfway through.

Some of the greatest authors of all time have mastered pacing in different ways:

- **Jane Austen (Pride and Prejudice)** – Balances witty, fast-paced dialogue with slow-burning emotional tension, making every exchange meaningful.

- **Leo Tolstoy (War and Peace)** – Alternates between rapid, chaotic war scenes and slow, introspective character moments, mirroring the ebb and flow of real life.

- **James Baldwin (Go Tell It on the Mountain)** – Uses long, immersive passages for deep emotional introspection, slowing the pacing to highlight character struggles.

- **Raymond Chandler (The Big Sleep)** – Keeps detective fiction sharp and fast-paced, cutting out excess description and making every word count.

- **Toni Morrison (Beloved)** – Slows down pivotal emotional moments with rich, lyrical prose, ensuring the weight of each revelation is fully felt.

Pacing isn't just about speed, it's about controlling how a story unfolds to maximize suspense, deepen emotional impact, and keep readers hooked. Here's how to master it.

1. Vary the Pacing to Match the Tone, Slow for Emotional Moments, Fast for Action.

The pacing of your story should align with its emotional tone and the type of scene you're writing. In emotionally charged moments, allow the pacing to slow down, giving readers space to absorb the weight of the scene. For example, a character reflecting on a loss or experiencing a quiet moment of self-discovery might require a slower pace to allow for introspection. On the flip side, action scenes — like a chase or a battle — need to move quickly. Use rapid-fire pacing to increase the sense of urgency, building momentum that pulls the reader through the scene. By varying the pacing in this way, you create a dynamic rhythm that keeps readers engaged, ensuring each scene has the right emotional impact.

When to slow the pacing:

- **For emotional depth** – Let readers absorb big moments, whether it's heartbreak, realization, or grief.

    Example: In Anna Karenina, Tolstoy lingers over Anna's emotional turmoil before her final decision, forcing the reader to sit in her despair.

- **For building suspense** – Slowly unravel information to increase tension before a reveal.

    Example: Daphne du Maurier's Rebecca gradually unveils the dark secrets of Manderley, making the revelations even more shocking.

- **For creating atmosphere** – Take time to set the scene and immerse the reader in a world.

    Example: In Wuthering Heights, Emily Brontë describes the moors in long, stormy passages that mirror the characters' emotional turmoil.

When to speed up the pacing:

- **During action sequences** – Short, sharp sentences mimic quick movements and rising tension.

Example: Ernest Hemingway in For Whom the Bell Tolls writes battle scenes with crisp, no-frills prose to mirror the intensity of combat.

- **During moments of urgency** – If a character is in danger, the pace should mirror their adrenaline.

    Example: In Dracula, Bram Stoker uses journal entries with clipped, anxious descriptions to make the vampire hunts feel frantic.

- **During arguments or high-conflict dialogue** – Rapid back-and-forth exchanges create energy and momentum.

    Example: F. Scott Fitzgerald's The Great Gatsby speeds up pacing in Gatsby's final confrontation with Tom Buchanan, making their tension feel volatile and electric.

How to apply this in your writing:

1. Match pacing to emotion: fast for excitement, slow for contemplation.
2. Use description length to control rhythm: detailed for slow pacing, concise for fast.
3. Pay attention to dialogue: quick exchanges increase pace, long pauses slow it down.

2. Keep Your Chapters or Scenes Moving with Purpose.

Every scene or chapter should move the story forward. Even quieter, slower moments should serve a purpose, whether it's deepening character relationships, revealing important backstory, or setting up future conflict. Avoid dragging scenes out for the sake of filling pages. If a scene doesn't contribute to the plot or character development, it's time to tighten it up or remove it. In action-heavy sequences, you want the pacing to feel continuous, with each paragraph leading to the next without pause. Even in quieter moments, ensure that each action, piece of dialogue, or thought pushes the narrative in a meaningful direction. This sense of purposeful movement keeps the story from feeling stagnant.

How to keep pacing tight and purposeful:

- **Start scenes late, leave early** – Don't waste time with mundane details; enter just as something interesting happens.

    Example: Elmore Leonard's crime novels open in the middle of the action, cutting out unnecessary buildup.

- **Avoid unnecessary exposition** – Trust the reader to fill in blanks without overloading them with background information.

    Example: In Invisible Man, Ralph Ellison reveals backstory naturally through character experiences rather than dumping information all at once.

- **Balance action with reflection** – Even in fast-paced genres like thrillers, moments of introspection give readers a chance to catch their breath.

    Example: In One Hundred Years of Solitude, Gabriel García Márquez interweaves magical realism with slower, poetic passages that explore generational trauma.

Examples of stories that maintain purposeful pacing:

- **In Crime and Punishment,** Dostoevsky alternates between slow psychological introspection and moments of intense action, reflecting Raskolnikov's unstable mind.

- **In The Stranger,** Albert Camus' detached prose makes fast-paced, shocking moments feel even more jarring.

- **In The Sun Also Rises,** Hemingway keeps his pacing crisp, cutting unnecessary words to maintain a steady, engaging flow.

How to apply this in your writing:

1. Ask: Does this scene move the story forward? If not, cut or condense it.
2. Trim excess descriptions. Long passages should contribute to atmosphere, not stall the plot.
3. Use dialogue and action to propel pacing forward.

3. Use Short Sentences and Paragraphs for Tension.

When you want to build tension or suspense, pacing is key. One way to achieve this is by using shorter sentences and paragraphs. This technique creates a faster reading pace, which ramps up tension and urgency. It's especially effective during moments of conflict, surprise, or danger. The fragmented feel of quick sentences mimics the rapid, heightened emotional state of your characters, creating a visceral experience for the reader. The break from longer, more detailed paragraphs also makes each moment feel sharper, heightening the anticipation and drawing readers in even further.

How short sentences build tension:

- **They mimic fast, desperate thoughts.**

  Example: "He ran. He stumbled. He turned the corner. The shadow followed."

- **They create abruptness.**

  Example: "The phone rang. She hesitated. Picked it up. No answer."

- **They feel like a heartbeat accelerating.**

  Example: "She heard the noise again. Closer. Louder. The door creaked."

Examples of pacing through sentence structure:

- **William Faulkner (As I Lay Dying)** – Uses long, stream-of-consciousness sentences for introspection and fragmented lines for chaos.

- **Shirley Jackson (The Lottery)** – Starts slow and descriptive, then cuts sentences shorter and sharper as the tension builds toward the shocking twist.

- **Franz Kafka (The Metamorphosis)** – Uses meandering descriptions to slow time, contrasting with sudden, sharp moments of transformation.

How to apply this in your writing:

1. Use short sentences and paragraphs in moments of action, fear, or intensity.
2. Lengthen descriptions when the mood is reflective or slow.
3. Play with sentence rhythm to create contrast between calm and chaos.

TIP 50. HOW TO WRITE A STORY THAT RESONATES WITH YOUR AUDIENCE

A truly unforgettable story doesn't just entertain, it connects, resonates, and lingers in the mind, causing the readers see themselves or the world differently. The stories that stand the test of time don't rely solely on plot twists or clever dialogue, they resonate because they tap into universal emotions, unforgettable characters, and themes that reflect the human experience.

Some of the most impactful stories across literature, film, and television have endured because they speak to deeply personal and universal truths:

- **Victor Hugo (*Les Misérables*)** – Explores themes of justice, redemption, and human resilience, making readers question morality and compassion.

- **Maya Angelou (*I Know Why the Caged Bird Sings*)** – A deeply personal yet universal story of overcoming hardship, self-acceptance, and finding one's voice.

- **John Steinbeck (*The Grapes of Wrath*)** – Captures the struggles of the working class, displacement, and the pursuit of dignity, themes that remain relevant across generations.

- **Chimamanda Ngozi Adichie (*Half of a Yellow Sun*)** – Weaves a deeply personal story of love and war, exploring the weight of history and personal sacrifice.

- **Alan Moore (*Watchmen*)** – Deconstructs the idea of heroism, power, and moral ambiguity, forcing readers to reconsider the true cost of justice.

Stories that resonate make readers feel something real, something that speaks to their own fears, hopes, struggles, and dreams. Here's how to create a story that leaves a lasting impact.

1. Tap into Universal Themes and Emotions.

Great stories often explore themes that transcend time, culture, and individual experiences, things like love, loss, identity, betrayal, and hope. These universal themes are relatable to anyone, no matter where they come from or what their personal background is. For example, a story about overcoming adversity, finding belonging, or discovering one's purpose resonates because these are feelings and experiences most people can relate to on some level. Use these themes to connect with your readers emotionally, creating a story that speaks to their hearts and experiences. When your story explores these universal truths, it becomes more than just a narrative, it becomes a reflection of the human condition.

How to use universal themes effectively:

- **Show characters struggling with emotions readers recognize** – Loneliness, joy, grief, longing, ambition.

    Example: In Les Misérables, Victor Hugo explores the theme of justice vs. mercy, making readers question their own moral beliefs.

- **Explore big questions through intimate moments** – Make complex themes personal through character-driven narratives.

Example: In The Picture of Dorian Gray, Oscar Wilde tackles vanity and morality through the intimate corruption of one man's soul.

- **Use simple, relatable truths** — Often, it's the smallest moments that carry the deepest weight.

   Example: In A Tree Grows in Brooklyn, Betty Smith captures the bittersweet pain of growing up through small, everyday struggles.

Examples of stories built on universal themes:

- **Emily Dickinson's poetry** — Themes of death, nature, and love, making her work timeless.

- **Franz Kafka's The Trial** — Captures anxiety and powerlessness, emotions that still resonate today.

- **Chinua Achebe's Things Fall Apart** — Examines cultural change, colonialism, and identity, making readers reflect on history and personal heritage.

How to apply this in your writing:

1. Ask: What fundamental human emotions or struggles am I exploring?
2. Make big themes personal by rooting them in your characters' experiences.
3. Don't force complexity — even simple, universal themes can carry immense power when done right.

2. Create Relatable Characters that Readers Can Connect With.

The characters are the heart of your story, and if readers can't connect with them, the story will fall flat. Create characters who feel real, with their own flaws, desires, and struggles. These characters don't need to be perfect, but they should be multidimensional, with motivations that drive their actions and decisions. Readers need to see parts of themselves in these characters, whether it's through shared emotions, dreams, or challenges. Show your characters in moments of vulnerability, making them relatable in both their strengths and their weaknesses. This connection allows readers to invest emotionally in the story, rooting for the characters as they navigate their journeys.

How to create characters that resonate:

- **Make them struggle with personal challenges** – A character's journey should reflect the fears, hopes, and insecurities readers recognize.

  Example: In The Bell Jar, Sylvia Plath's protagonist grapples with mental illness, making her struggle deeply relatable to many.

- **Give them real flaws, not just quirks** – A character who is *too perfect* feels inauthentic; give them internal conflicts that challenge them.

  Example: In Madame Bovary, Gustave Flaubert creates a deeply flawed heroine whose desires and choices feel painfully real.

- **Let them evolve in a way that feels earned** – Growth should come through experience, not convenience.

Example: In Crime and Punishment, Raskolnikov's gradual transformation makes his arc all the more powerful.

Examples of deeply relatable characters:

- **Elizabeth Bennet (Pride and Prejudice)** – Struggles with prejudice and self-awareness, making her personal growth feel real.

- **Holden Caulfield (The Catcher in the Rye)** – A character alienated from the world, making him relatable to anyone who's ever felt lost.

- **Jay Gatsby (The Great Gatsby)** – Represents the universal longing for an unattainable dream, making his story tragic and poignant.

How to apply this in your writing:

1. Ask: Does my character's struggle reflect a real human emotion?
2. Avoid stereotypes or clichés. Real people are complex, your characters should be too.
3. Ensure characters' choices and growth feel natural, not forced.

3. Make Your Story Meaningful. Leave Your Readers Thinking.

A story that resonates isn't just about entertainment, it has layers of meaning that linger long after the final page. Think about the questions you want to leave with your readers. What do you want them to reflect on after they've finished? Whether it's the way love changes us, the impact of our choices, or the complexities of human relationships, a meaningful story challenges readers to think deeper. Don't be afraid to introduce subtle layers of complexity or ambiguity. A story that gives readers something to think about - something that makes them reevaluate their own experiences or beliefs - will stay with them much longer than one that doesn't. Strive to create an experience that leaves an emotional imprint, one that resonates with readers in ways that go beyond the surface.

How to make your story meaningful:

- **Ask a deep question—but don't provide easy answers** – Stories that linger often leave space for interpretation.

    Example: In Waiting for Godot, Samuel Beckett doesn't give clear answers, making readers reflect on existential meaning.

- **Create moments that feel universally true** – A single sentence, a piece of dialogue, or a character's realization can hit hard if it speaks to something real.

    Example: In Of Mice and Men, Steinbeck's final moment between George and Lennie is gut-wrenching because it speaks to sacrifice and love in its rawest form.

- **Use subtext to add layers** – A powerful story doesn't always state its meaning outright; it lets readers discover it.

    Example: In Beloved, Toni Morrison reveals trauma in fragments, forcing the reader to put the emotional puzzle together.

Examples of stories that leave readers thinking:

- **George Eliot's Middlemarch** – Explores marriage, ambition, and regret, resonating because it reflects real-life complexities.

- **Gabriel García Márquez's Love in the Time of Cholera** – A love story that questions the very nature of time, desire, and obsession.

- **Margaret Atwood's The Handmaid's Tale** – Leaves readers questioning power, control, and gender politics, long after they finish.

How to apply this in your writing:

1. Ask: What do I want my readers to take away from this?
2. Let thematic weight emerge naturally, rather than forcing a "message."
3. Consider leaving room for ambiguity — some of the best stories don't wrap everything up neatly.

CONCLUSION: YOUR JOURNEY AS A WRITER HAS ONLY JUST BEGUN

Writing is not just about words on a page — it's about telling stories that matter, stories that connect, inspire, and endure. As you've journeyed through *The Writer's Compass: 50 Tips to Help Navigate Your Storytelling Journey*, I hope you've found guidance, inspiration, and the confidence to keep pushing forward in your creative endeavors.

Every writer faces doubts. Every writer encounters roadblocks. But the difference between those who dream of writing and those who become writers is simple: persistence. Whether you're refining your craft, building compelling characters, mastering pacing, or finding ways to make your story truly resonate — every step you take makes you a stronger storyteller.

You now have a toolkit of insights, strategies, and hard-earned wisdom from the greatest storytellers of the past and present. But remember: writing is an evolving craft. You will continue to learn, to grow, and to refine your voice. The best thing you can do? Keep writing. Keep experimenting. Keep telling the stories only you can tell.

The world needs your voice. The world needs your stories.

So, pick up your pen, open your laptop, and start again.

Your next great story is waiting.

NOTE FROM THE AUTHOR

First and foremost, thank you for taking the time to read *The Writer's Compass: 50 Tips to Help Navigate Your Storytelling Journey*. Writing this book has been an incredible experience, and my hope is that it has inspired, motivated, and helped you grow as a writer. Whether you're just starting out or refining your craft, I want you to know that your stories matter, and your voice is important.

If you found this book helpful, insightful, or inspiring, I'd truly appreciate it if you could take a moment to leave a five-star review on Amazon, Goodreads, or wherever you purchased this book. Reviews make a huge difference — they help other writers and storytellers discover these tips and techniques and allow me to continue creating content that supports and uplifts the writing community. Your feedback not only helps the book reach more people, but it also means the world to me as an author.

I'd also love for you to share this book with fellow writers, friends, or anyone passionate about storytelling. If you know someone who's struggling with writer's block, crafting their first novel, or simply looking for creative inspiration, send them this book! Writing is a journey best traveled with others, and your recommendation can help another writer overcome challenges and reignite their creative spark.

Beyond this book, I'm always looking to connect with writers, readers, and fellow creatives. You can follow me on Instagram and TikTok at @MichaelMWrites for more writing tips, creative inspiration, and behind-the-scenes insights into the writing process. I love engaging with my community, answering questions, and seeing how other writers bring their ideas to life. Feel free to tag me in your posts, share your favorite takeaways from the book, and introduce yourself — I'd love to hear from you!

If you have questions, want to collaborate, or simply want to chat about storytelling, you can always reach me at Michael@MichaelMWrites.com. Whether you're looking for writing advice, have feedback on the book, or want to share your latest project, I'd love to connect and support you on your journey.

Once again, thank you for being part of this creative adventure. Writing isn't always easy, but it's one of the most rewarding and powerful forms of self-expression. Keep writing, keep dreaming, and most importantly — keep sharing your stories with the world.

Happy writing!

Michael Mammarella

www.ingramcontent.com/pod-product-compliance
Lightning Source LLC
Chambersburg PA
CBHW071958070526
44583CB00015B/1243